HUSTLE
WITH
HEART

Unlocking Self-Worth through
Personal Trust Communities

Mike Thorne

Published by Mindstir Media, LLC
45 Lafayette Rd | Suite 181| North Hampton, NH 03862 | USA
1.800.767.0531 | www.mindstirmedia.com

Printed in the United States of America
ISBN-13: 978-1-958729-69-4 (paperback)

DEDICATION

There are so many that have shaped me, pushed me, and supported me throughout my life and wanted to note them below.

To mom & dad—your love, caring nature, and support throughout my life has meant so much.

Dad—Hopefully you can get a copy of this up in heaven but, if not, know that connecting me to sports (both watching and participating) has catapulted me in life on so many levels and I thank you for that.

Mom, the family ROCK, your relentless drive (even with a walker you want to go faster than most), and the ability to overcome life's obstacles has spurred me to keep learning and growing. Know I love and appreciate you to the moon and back.

Alice, I know this book has taken longer than we both hoped (your gallow humor about dying before I finish has been so on "brand" now that I know you") yet here it is. I wouldn't be on this earth and none of this wouldn't even be possible without the courage and conviction you showed almost 58 years ago.

Brother Vinnie who like all good older brothers would take me out with friends or let me hang out with him despite the fact that I usually was a bump on the log and never great company. Thanks for still being the big brother I call today to discuss important topics and family life. I am grateful we still stay connected and watch out for each other.

Debbie, my sister, for just being there for me allowing us to be vulnerable and sharing life's challenges, laughing through some and reflecting on others.

Sometimes as an older brother I do wish I was more aware of what was happening "back in the day" and how I could have been there more often yet also believe we have grown closer as we get older which I so value.

And to my wife, best friend, and mother to our children, Maggie. I don't even know what to say without writing a chapter about our entire journey but I will keep it short because you are never one who wants to be in the limelight, yet one who deserves to be. I will never forget junior year in college when you walked out of our townhouse and I thought to myself, "wow, that is the girl I would love to marry." Who knew how the next 35+ years would unfold!

We "formally" met in Maryland and had our first "date" in the Inner Harbor and next to a Bullets (now Wizards)—Celtics game where Larry Bird wins with a 3 point shot in double overtime. You were brave enough to visit my lovely 2 bedroom "condo" with yellow and orange walls (my color choice for condos was never a sweet spot, remember all the blue in Schaumburg?) and test my grilled chicken which is still a specialty today (Ha) and here we are over 35+ years later. How did I get so lucky and blessed to have you on this journey with me? For someone who didn't trust easily, worried about being abandoned, and being perfect, somehow you saw through all that and over our 32+ year marriage you helped shape me and challenged me to be a better husband, father, friend, boss, and human being. Each time I needed a nudge, find the right words, or a hand you have been there. I will be forever grateful and look forward to our next chapters together.

Our daughters—Amanda, Sarah and Katie, each of you has and will continue to be a blessing and inspiration to me and others. Your dad tried his best along the way yet it was all of you that shaped me, helped me see other perspectives, and see the power of being others focused. Never letting me get too high or too low, yet always providing examples of your compassion and caring natures that helped me so much.

Amanda teaching your father patience, gratitude, and above all compassion as I learned what it took to be a father and parent. I loved those dance recitals (senior year video tribute to your folks while sitting in our bedroom chair surprise still brings tears to my eyes even as I write this) watching Gilmore Girls with you (Luke is still my favorite), going to country music concerts (especially Thomas Rhett and having him sing Beer with Jesus thanks to you,), Shania Twain and others. Red Sox games (remember that 16 inning game that ended at 1:30am?) are memories a daughter and dad will always have. Seeing you now as a grown woman positively impacting people with your work is inspiring me to be a better human being and father, and I will be forever grateful for that.

Sarah "teaching" you to jump off the kitchen counter on a 1–2–3 cadence and then "catching" you when you were very little (probably not something in the parent playbook.) Your infectious laugh, playing catch with the baseball in the front yard (solving all of life's challenges!), going to your dance recitals and watching you grow up each year with them. Your High School musicals and watching you go to college and growing from a small town girl to a "city" girl. Your work as a teacher and pushing for women's rights, standing up for yourself, and holding your dad accountable to fully understand the racial and inequities in society. Thank you for making me a better father and human being kid.

Katie—Our youngest, kiddingly calling you the family dog while growing up as you were always willing to hop in the car and go anywhere. Playing tennis together, watching the Sports Reporters on Sunday, going to the Stanley Cup finals in Nashville with the Predators. Building a business that focuses on STEM education for Special Needs kids (having you call us to be the initial investor in your "business" was impressive!) are all moments that are seared in my mind. You have a gift of seeing the best in others, especially those who society has marginalized. Your compassion, sense of humor, and inner drive to be the best are gifts we all can learn from.

Sister Kimberly and brother Duane, although we didn't grow up together, you two are an inspiration to me. You have done so much to take care of each other and your families are so connected. I am at times jealous I wasn't there growing up with you yet also so appreciative of the time we have had these last 10+ years.

Father John for all the wisdom you shared, for being there with our family in good times and difficult times, you have taught me so much. My life is so much richer for having you in it. Tim Dixon, teaching me gratitude, guiding me from doing what I need to do to what I want to do was so instrumental to my growth over the last 5+ years.

Kevin Clayton who shaped my thinking on diversity and inclusion since my time at Russell Athletic in 2005–2006 while on the company Diversity team. I am forever grateful for your teachings and ability to force us to have the difficult conversations that are so necessary in organizations for them to thrive. I always draw on my experience and I am grateful we met.

Sheila Brennan Nee, we have only known each other for less than 5 years yet it feels like a lifetime. Your genuine interest in my life and family and your ability to care so deeply is extraordinary and so happy to have you in my life. Our shared interest in sports, family and life makes our conversations so freeing.

Toraire Durden, constantly challenging my thinking and always being there to discuss lifes lessons. Fred Kelley for teaching me what being a best friend means and how to be a lifelong godfather (and to Michelle who makes Katie feel special)

Martha Lacroix—You have stood by since I interviewed with you in 2006 to this day and I am forever grateful. When I was in grief when losing a key employee in a tragic accident you were there to share wisdom and other times we shared a lot of laughs as well, truly a friend indeed. Craig Rydin and Harlan thanks for taking a chance on me and teaching me how to lead from the heart while still delivering on the financial obligations of a business.

Jeff Fiorini—Back in 1987 you were a colleague and "competitor" as a young sales person with Wilson yet over time became a mentor, friend, confidante and for Maggie and I, you and Lisa best friends. The kind of friend who knows what to say in the right way at the right time so it lands well and that is a gift. I have lost more money playing golf with you than won, shared more laughs to a point of tears, and enjoyed kicking your ass in basketball yet at all points left time with you a better friend, father, husband and dad and I thank you.

Robert Lewis who taught me the power of conviction and a relentless belief that everyone deserves the opportunities for access and resources so they can thrive. You are a force of nature and someone I look to for inspiration when life seems to throw you a curveball, I always think of you. Thanks for being in my life.

Carl Ferraro who taught me life lessons along with how to be a professional. Bill Kirchner, a mentor and business leader who gave me a foundation to be a professional salesperson and business leader that I am forever grateful for. I still tell people stories of what you did for me, and I thank you for the selfless teachings "back in the day"

Dorrin Exford, who I met in 2006 at Yankee Candle. Your ability to be others focused and care for them is a leadership model we need more of. Outside of family, there has been no one that I can think of that has transformed me more as a human being. Dorrin, your energy, ability to see through people to find their gifts and bring it out of them is something I have admired and tried to bring to my relationships over the last 20+ years of my life. I will forever be grateful for all you have done for me.

DISCLAIMERS

I love to read fables that teach lessons through the story versus giving an A to Z lesson on how to be the best human being in the world. When I started this it was how I wanted to approach it except instead of it being a fable, it was a real story and person. My intention is that those who read it, pick up the nuances and lessons throughout each chapter and maybe find a nugget or two and apply it to their life and ultimately become a better person because of it.

In this book, I did my best to remember and recreate events and conversations while bringing context for the times they happened. In some cases, I used the actual names of people because I felt it told the story best while also hopefully helping share lessons for those who are reading this book. I learned something from everyone in this book and in some cases I wish I could go back in time and replay the events over and have a better outcome. Unfortunately that isn't possible and it also isn't how life works.

In other cases, the names of people or companies were not used yet sharing the "lesson" or story was important to "teach" those who are reading it as they navigate their life and career. I am confident those who were there or know the stories might see the events or lessons differently and that is why being a father, husband, friend and business leader is so hard. Words, actions, and body language really matter yet many of us (myself included) didn't understand or take the time to pause and truly understand the impact of our actions, words or approach to the situations captured in the book.

Finally, this book was written from my perspective and I respect that others might have seen or experienced things differently or remembered events and timing differently. I also expect that some may disagree with some of the sections and the stories in the book.

I want people to read this as a true story yet one that helps them reflect on their own life and maybe inspires them to see where they played a role in their ups and downs and begin to assess their own actions and ultimately to become an "others" focused human being. Hopefully this book inspires others to build their North Star and Personal Trust Community so that they don't live their life under someone else's terms.

ACKNOWLEDGEMENTS:

Thank you to everyone who had a hand in making this book reality. Bryan Wish, it all started with a simple note on LI related to a post and here we are almost 2 years later and Arcbound and your entire team have been fantastic partners. A blessing to meet Carson Morell—the wizard behind the curtain making sure all aspects of our relationship and the book work well.

Without a doubt, Ariel Hubbard is the main reason this book ever got done and she made sense of our many Zoom calls, e-mails, and texts throughout the last 12+ months. Her experience, ability to roll with the ups and downs of my demeanor and level of frustration throughout was essential to get this done. She was able to help me put my thoughts into words and bring the story to life.

More importantly, her challenges, questions, and intellectual curiosity forced me to reckon with so many layers of my life. I feel like the entire process was therapy for me and I am blessed to have her in my life. Thanks for all the time, energy, and effort Arial!

Morgan Beavers you are amazing, knowing how to read my mind/thoughts and push me out of my comfort zone as I reconcile my past and where I want to go in the future. Kit Maier—your patience with me is to be commended, Ashley Merdinger you are an old soul and you have a way of sharing feedback that hits home but feels so genuine, thank you for all the support.

Aaron Mosby, silent yet such a powerful force in helping me get a feel for how to bring myself to the world through the book and website, thank you!

I love how you pushed me beyond my comfort zone. Marji Shrimpton, your passion and energy kept me going throughout the book journey even when I didn't want to.

Rich Keller—I wouldn't have even had the confidence, belief in myself, or language to get this book off the ground without you pushing and challenging me to find my one word. You have literally transformed the way I show up in the world. To identify what this PTC really is and to stay focused on the outcome when I just wanted it to all go away. I tried so hard to quit or make you stop trying to help me, yet your relentlessness and genuine interest in helping me share an authentic voice as a Transformer was instrumental in getting this project off the ground.

Jodi Villani—You always had a great eye on design and a feel for who I am and your perspective on the cover and how it ties to me meant so much and I am so grateful to have you in my life.

To Debbie Levasseur, my sister, for putting up with me while I tried to remember aspects of our childhood. All the calls, texting, emailing at all hours and days of the week to confirm accuracy. Your support was immense and I am grateful to have you in my life and thank you for putting up with me during the book writing process. Did I really have a "crush" on a girl when I was 5? I digress, but the level of detail you remembered was extraordinary and likely could fit another book.

To all of you, thank you so much.

Our home on Blueberry Lane in Sturbridge

INTRODUCTION

I want to tell you a story.

When I was nine years old, my parents delivered some life-altering news—news that made me feel as if I could only count on myself, and that, if I wasn't perfect, I could easily be left behind. I took those feelings to heart.

My mindset revolved around solving my own problems, and doing so flawlessly, resulting in professional and personal success—until it didn't. And despite all of the early successes, I felt unfulfilled and alone most if not all of the time. And it not only affected the way I showed up in the world, but it also influenced every decision I made and every transformation I weathered.

For a long time, I made choices in my personal life that held me back. I shielded who I was and took jobs—although they were logical steps and grew my "resume"—to prove my worth to the world. I felt as if I had to control my decisions and destiny or it could all be taken away. Combined with a strong desire to fit in and show others my value, those choices undermined me in so many ways. I took lefts when I should have made rights, because I didn't know how to ask for help. Plus, I didn't trust anyone enough to feel comfortable. I worried that showing vulnerability would also make me vulnerable to being left behind. Not a great way to show up personally or professionally.

Here's the thing, though: life is all about transformations. We're constantly evaluating where we are and determining where to go next. And for all of us, there are numerous factors that have an impact on the decisions we make—not just our hopes and dreams, but our anxieties, ideas about the world and what it means to be successful, and the expectations of our loved ones. With so many factors to sift through, it's easy to get off track. It's easy to start following someone else's North Star or take a roundabout route to arrive at your own. But it doesn't have to be that way.

Over the course of my life and career, I identified a process that must unfold during any successful transition. I call it "Belong, Build, Believe." It's the idea that **we must *belong*, or feel as if we're a part of a team, organization, or community, before we can *build* the confidence necessary to contribute the best of what we have to offer, and ultimately *believe* in our success.**

In working with thousands of people, I've learned that everyone has one thing in common, regardless of their background. **When someone doesn't feel like they belong, they won't have the confidence to bring their whole self to the table, and instead of committing to a business or a relationship, they will be compliant.**

Further, building confidence is a continuous process that always comes back to belonging. **Believing in ourselves requires us to continually remind ourselves that we're capable—and have others reinforce that we belong, too.**

And while it sounds counterintuitive and many of us would like to think otherwise, **believing in ourselves often requires having someone else believe in us first.**

Having a community that supports us helps us get to our goals faster, because community reminds us that we aren't alone in our struggles. Eventually, I learned that I could make better decisions, bring more value to the table, and do it much quicker when I consulted trusted members of my community. And more than that, I had to seek out the right people for help addressing the right issues. I had to build a Personal Trust Community—people on whom I could rely for different issues.

For instance, some of my best college friends were great at building me up when I needed it but maybe not ideal resources for specific business challenges for which they didn't have context. Childless colleagues could help me navigate a salary conversation, but they couldn't provide valuable insights on how to find harmony between my responsibilities in the office with those at home. Nor should I go to the people who I knew would only tell me what I wanted to hear. Instead, I had to ask those who understood my conundrum and could provide a thoughtful and objective perspective.

When I realized that, everything clicked. **There's truly nothing better than having human beings in your life who will grab you by the arm and say, "You've got this."** Those who are honest with you and aren't afraid to say when you've taken a wrong step because they trust in your ability to bounce back.

I didn't learn these lessons in the classroom. I learned through trial and error. It took me a long time to put it all together, to make decisions with intention and rely on the right bench strength. But once I understood how much my relationships could enrich my life—and that the two most important phrases in the English language are "I love you" and "I need help"—I found myself heading in the right direction. **I had to hustle, yes, but I could do it with heart, letting others support me along the way.**

I was adjusting as needed, and making my plays count, because I had a game plan and the right teammates to make it happen. **Sometimes, you need to let the game come to you too.**

I also realized that I learned the most when I took the time to listen to people at work or home, asking them to tell me their story. At the office, I'd walk around with a notepad and pen and write down what they said. When they opened up, I could understand what they'd been through, what they could bring to the table, and how I could help. It wasn't textbooks or trainings that taught me what I needed to know; it was real human interactions.

That's what I'm offering you here. I'm sharing my story in the hope that it resonates. I hope that it helps you work through your struggles and access your greatness more efficiently. I hope it drives home how important you are, and how powerful your relationships can be—both personally and professionally.

And when you're ready to talk, I'm here.

Suggestions for Speaker:

Speaker Name: _Mike Thorne_

Comments from: _Dorrin_

This is an informal evaluation for speakers of the evening. You will be given time after their speech to record your comments. Evaluations help you become a better listener, and help the speaker with positive comments and helpful suggestions.

1. **What strengths or potential strengths were displayed which should be maintained and built upon?**

   Great contact w/ audiance
   — Sincerity —
   — Openness and Clear sense of purpose
   — Good eye contact
   — Well developed —
   — Nicely executed — in 3rd Person —

2. **Describe any elements or areas for improvement, caution or fine-tuning.**

   Your time is so limited — I know
   with additional practice
   you would not have needed
   notes —

   Great first job
                    Congrats.

   (also — extremely interesting life
   story!)

Yankee Candle Event that changed my life

CHAPTER 1

"If you trust, you don't worry. If you worry, you don't trust."
—Unknown

I finally decided to make the call. Forty-six years was long enough.

I held my breath as the phone rang once, twice. I had spent years thinking about what I'd say when she answered, but when the call patched through and a man picked up, I found myself tongue-tied.

"Hello, this is Russell," he said then paused, waiting for my response.

I cleared my throat. "I, uh, I was looking to speak to Alice…"

"She's not here," he said, "can you call back tomorrow?" I was so flustered I hung up without answering. But I promised myself I'd follow through. Tomorrow, I would call back.

The next day, I picked up the phone again. This time, I had done more to prepare, writing down exactly what I was going to say.

And this time, after the second ring, a woman answered. I looked at the script in front of me. "Hi," I started, "my name is Mike Thorne, and I believe Alice is my mother. I'm calling to thank her for what she did."

In that moment, I felt the weight of everything I'd been carrying dissipate. *There, I said it!* I thought.

It didn't matter what happened next. The hardest part of my job was done. I'd found my biological mother, reached out to her, and offered up the one message I knew I needed to share.

Long ago, I'd surrendered to the reality that I may never find my biological parents, or that they wouldn't want to talk to or see me once I did locate them. Even when I picked up the phone, I worried about being rejected once again—the first time, I reasoned, being when my mother had given me up at birth. But when the call went through and I offered my gratitude, that all went away.

Meanwhile, I was met with silence. In the seven seconds it took for the woman on the other side of the line to gather her thoughts, time seemed to slow.

Finally, she introduced herself. "I'm Kimberly," she said. "I've heard about you, but I can't believe I'm actually talking to you. I always wondered what happened to you—I'm so glad you called." She paused. "I don't know if Alice will want to speak with you, but I'm your sister, and I would like to." She gave me her phone number and told me she'd be out shopping with our mother tomorrow, and that she'd ask Alice what she wanted to do. And just like that, the call was over.

I closed my eyes, trying to picture what Alice looked like. I wondered what she'd say when she heard the news and—above all—whether she would want to talk to me or maybe even see me.

* * *

I remember the day I got another life-changing call, one that would kick off so much transformation—both personally and professionally. I had been given the opportunity to change industries from the father of one of my daughter's friends—a job as president of the wholesale division at Yankee Candle Company.

With twenty years in sporting goods, I was an unlikely candidate—even more so because they had been looking for someone who had worked in home decor and fragrance space. I didn't know the man who recommended me well, but he was well-respected by the search firm looking to fill the role and must have spoken highly of me, and that was enough to secure a video conference call.

This was in 2005, before video conferencing was an everyday occurrence, and I remember driving to an office with the technology necessary to join the call. It was right when LifeSize was around (maybe Skype?) and just before MySpace came out. After three or four months of interviews and logistics, I was finally offered the job. Although my initial interview with my future boss had only included time for one question, that question landed well. He asked me about the most important lesson I'd learned from my experience with my past employer, Russell Athletic.

I responded, "If senior leadership isn't aligned on the mission and direction of a business, it will struggle and fail to achieve success." It was honest and all I had to say. Apparently, it was enough.

And while my wife was worried about me leaving the sporting goods industry after so many years, I was eager for the change. Yankee Candle had a warm, family-business feel—so different from the male-dominated sporting goods world, where showing emotion was cast as a weakness. Right away, I knew I loved the people who worked there. And just about a year later, I'd have a meeting with a woman there who would change my life.

Dorrin Exford was Yankee Candle's director of learning and development. When I first met her, I was immediately struck by the power of her presence. She was highly experienced and older than me but seemed to have the energy of someone fifteen years my junior, with a great smile and an infectious laugh. I could sense her passion, drive, and sales skills almost instantly, but her true expertise lay in making those she talked to feel seen and heard. When you were with Dorrin, she made it all about you. She recently told me that early on, she sensed that I had a question in my head: *If people really knew me, would they still like me?* She decided right then and there that she needed to help me. She felt I had a hole in me, and she wanted to help fill it.

About a year after I'd been there, she came into my office. "Well," she started, "I've got good news and bad news."

She told me that the leadership team had been curious as to whether I could make the switch from sporting goods to a business where the core consumer was female, a lot of women held key positions, and thus where there was an entirely different culture—alongside an entirely different product category.

"So," I said, "What's the good news?"

"The good news is in your first year here, you've become a very approachable senior executive. Everyone feels very comfortable coming to talk to you one on one."

"Great, what's the bad news?"

"Your standards are way too high."

I knew she was right. After all, I'd heard it before. Other colleagues had shared that the teams I led struggled to live up to the benchmarks I set. I knew where it came from, too.

I'd always been afraid of not being good enough. Perfection seemed to be the only way to guarantee personal and professional success. So, I demanded perfection from my team as well. And while they complied with what I asked them to do, they never really committed to me. As Dorrin explained, they just didn't feel like they could reach the bar I was setting, and that was discouraging. They felt as if they couldn't reach me, either.

"If you can just be vulnerable, if you can just let them know you have your own share of challenges, you can overcome that. Share some personal stories," she encouraged. "Talk about your kids, about what's going on in your life. If you do, I think you'll find you have a very different relationship with your team."

I nodded, weighing everything she was saying.

"Here's a tip. Every Monday morning, just walk the floor. Check in with people. See how their weekend was. And tell them something about yours."

It sounded simple enough. I agreed to try.

With her guidance, I began sharing small chunks of myself—taking a walk around the floor on Mondays and at times on Friday too. At that point, I was overseeing a team of more than 100 people, and I was astounded by how quickly we developed a rapport thanks to those check-ins. They would share what was happening in their lives, and I'd respond with stories of my own.

Eventually, I stopped worrying that they would think less of me if they saw too much, and when I did, I noticed that their performance began to improve. What had always seemed so distant began to come into focus.

Dorrin also recommended that I join the company's Toastmasters group, where I could get help finding my voice in a safe environment. Figuring I had nothing to lose, I began to attend.

And in 2010, while presenting to a group of the company's leaders as part of the Toastmasters program, about four years after I started at Yankee Candle and three years after that conversation with Dorrin, I decided to share even more. It wasn't easy; I'd always worried that if I let my guard down—if I let myself be vulnerable—I'd be abandoned.

In fact, I had only come to trust Dorrin because she first shared what she'd been through with me, recounting a childhood that had its own challenges. Knowing about her lived experience, I immediately felt a connection, trusting that she understood where I was coming from. She became my first "true" Personal Trust Community member from a professional standpoint. I'd never felt that way in the sporting goods industry. The personal stuff remained private; that's just the way it was. But I was ready for another change.

I told the office Toastmasters group that I had been adopted. I shared a bit about what that had meant for my life and the questions I had about my biological family.

Afterward, colleagues came up to me with their own stories. They revealed that they had been adopted as well, and they'd always wondered whether they should seek out their birth parents. Believe it or not, that was the first time I realized that there were a lot of people just like me.

A short while later, as I was contemplating trying to find my biological mom, I was approached by Craig Rydin, our CEO. I admired Craig personally and professionally. He had salt and pepper hair, kind eyes, and was quick to smile. Craig was like the heavy wool blanket you pull on during a cold New England winter night to help keep you warm. The sheer comfort of having it makes you sleep better, even if it can't quite cut through the chill. That was how Craig made me feel as a person and a leader. And he had a unique perspective on the challenges and complexities of finding one's biological parents. He and his wife had adopted a son, and he offered to share his thoughts on how to navigate a conversation with my adoptive parents.

"It sounds like you're ready to find your biological mother. But if you do decide to find her, you've got to understand the relationships that will be affected by that decision," he said.

"Your decision will have an impact on your biological mom, too," he added. "How is she going to feel if you suddenly show up at her door?"

We spent a couple hours together, talking through all of the dynamics involved in such a decision. It was helpful to hear his perspective, particularly since my parents had always been very hush hush about the whole thing. The story I'd been told was that one day, they got a phone call. A voice said, "We have a baby boy. Come get him." And that was that. I was theirs.

His insightful guidance gave me a new perspective along with confidence that I should proceed. In fact, after we finished, he looked at me and said, "I think it is time to find your mom."

And now that I'd shared the story at work, and that I'd gotten his perspective, I couldn't stop thinking about finding the woman who'd birthed me.

Soon after, I shared my plan with my wife and three daughters. They were immediately worried about how my parents would react. At that point, my parents were in their seventies, and they were nervous about the stress my decision would cause them. We agreed that it would be best if I told them up front, one on one, before I did anything else.

My family and I went to visit my parents in Maine to deliver the news. One night, we had a nice dinner at a local restaurant called The China Dine-ah in China, Maine, where they had a cottage. After the meal, my wife and daughters excused themselves, and I told my parents I had something I wanted to talk to them about—something very important to me.

Once we were alone, I cleared my throat. "I'd like to find my biological family," I said.

My mother looked down at her plate for a moment. Then, she said, "Does that mean I'm never going to see you again?"

My colleague had been right. At that point, I'd been their son for nearly forty-six years, and my mother had the same fears that he and his wife had experienced—that I'd connect with my biological family and leave the parents who raised me behind, never to return.

And had I not had that conversation with him before broaching the subject with my parents, I probably would have gotten very defensive. I may have said something I'd regret. But instead, I had some insight into where she was coming from. So, I took a different approach. "You've been amazing parents. And that's how I see you—as my parents. That won't change. But there's always been a hole in my heart. I just want to know who she is and what happened. It doesn't change our relationship or what you've meant to me. I just need to close a loop."

"I understand," my mother said finally, "but we don't have a lot of information to give you."

My adoption fell during a period known as the "Baby Scoop Era," which ran from around 1940–1970. Back then, the rate of premarital pregnancies increased as sexual norms began to change, access to birth control remained limited, and the stigma against "illegitimate children" held strong. The rate of newborn adoption rose accordingly, with an estimated 2 million mothers surrendering their babies during the 1960s alone.[1] Most adoptions were closed, as adoption organizations worried that birth parents might interfere with the child's life. So, my parents didn't know anything about the people who had given me up all those years ago. And unlike my colleague's son, who had been able to find his mother with a few clicks online, there weren't any readily available records of my adoption.

My best option was to reach out to a private investigator. Determined to find my biological mother, I connected with a company called OmniTrace, operating out of Florida. When I called and explained my situation, the person on the phone told me to keep in mind that they might never find my biological family. On the other hand, they might be able to track them down pretty quickly.

"You should be prepared for either outcome," he told me.

"I understand," I said. "By the way, what are the chances that my biological mother will want to talk to me if I do find her?" I asked.

He sighed. I pictured him leaning back in his desk chair, considering all he'd seen over the course of his career. "I'd say about 70 percent of the people that make the call have a good outcome; 30 percent not so much."

Those odds seemed good enough. I submitted my OmniTrace request on August 28. On October 13, an envelope arrived in the mail. I check the mail religiously, always have—every day for the past thirty-one years I've been married. It's as if I think I'm going to win the lottery, even though I don't play. It was surreal to see it sitting there, a different kind of lottery won.

I walked through the garage, into the family room, and then through to the kitchen, where my wife, Maggie, was working on a puzzle. I held up the envelope printed with OmniTrace's logo.

I'd had the past few months to think about how I'd react if and when the envelope arrived and what I'd do with the contents. I'd thought about making the call to my mother, about what I was going to say. I'd considered how I'd respond if she was happy to hear from me, and if she wasn't. I'd read books on adoption, including *Being Adopted: The Lifelong Search for Self*, and *Twenty Life Transforming Choices Adoptees Need to Make*. I'd talked to other senior leaders, as well as a former colleague of mine named Andrew, who had also been adopted.

Andrew had told me that when he finally met his biological family, he was stunned to see that he walked and talked just like his father. While I couldn't imagine what my parents looked like, I wondered if I walked like my father or talked like my mom. I pondered whether my father liked sports like I did, mulling over where the attributes that made me, me, had come from. Now, after a few short months and forty-six very long years, I was on the cusp of finding all of that out.

I had also thought about the reasons why my mother did what she did. My whole childhood, I believed she had just decided to get rid of me. But what if she had no choice? What if something tragic had happened? What if she couldn't possibly have taken care of me? Maybe she did the right thing.

Years later, I'd meet a man named Bo Eason, a former safety for the Houston Oilers, an actor, a playwright, and a motivational speaker who would help me think through so much of what had been running through my head. He'd express something that many others had mentioned in one way or another.

"Mike," he said, "I'm not trying to be crude here, but at any one time, there are 300 million sperm racing to be born. You already won that run. You won the first and hardest race you were ever in. Be grateful."

He was right and the others I'd met had been too—my mother could have made a different choice. Instead, I'd had a chance at life. I could have wound up in the foster care system, but instead I had great parents. And since then, I'd had the opportunity to pursue what I loved professionally and build a family of my own. I realized that instead of being pissed off at what had happened to me, I should consider myself blessed.

I decided that, more than anything, I should be grateful to my mother for doing what she did.

I headed into our home office and opened the envelope, spreading its contents across the desk. It held my birth certificate, and a page printed with some names and details about the people listed. They found a man who they thought was my father and pulled his obituary from the *Worcester Telegram & Gazette*. There, below it, was the name of the woman they believed to be my mother, along with her age, date of birth, address, and phone number. And below that was another name—a woman they listed as my sister. Her address was the same as my mother's. According to the document in front of me, they lived in Massachusetts, about an hour and a half from my home in Connecticut.

Soon, my wife appeared in the doorway. I showed her what they'd found. "What are you going to do?" she asked.

"I'm going to call and see what happens," I told her.

* * *

It was 1974. Nixon would resign, the Oakland A's would win the World Series, and I would turn ten years old that September. But the first important transformation of that year—at least in my world—happened during early spring.

My family lived in a split-level home on Blueberry Lane in Sturbridge, Massachusetts, about an hour from Boston. I'd spent the morning biking through the neighborhood with my friends before heading inside for a snack and some television. That time of year, the air still had a bite to it, and I felt my cheeks begin to thaw once I stepped inside.

"Honey," my mother called from the kitchen, "why don't you meet us in the family room?" It was the farthest room from the rest of the house—a typical seventies den, with wood paneling on the walls; thick, shaggy carpeting to match; and a big, boxy TV with tinfoil wrapped around the antenna. (We had three channels, plus channel 38—the sports network, so we could watch the Bruins, Celtics, and the Red Sox—none of which ever seemed to work. Hence, the foil).

I took my place on a beanbag chair, and my parents settled themselves across from me on the couch. They looked at each other for a bit and then turned their focus to me. "Well," my mother said, "we just wanted you to know that you're adopted, and we love you very much."

They nodded at each other, as if to say, *our work is done here*, as if it were a basic fact they needed to share. That was it. I was dismissed, and they got up as if nothing had happened.

But for me, it was as if a bomb went off. My life as I knew it has been blown to pieces. My feeling of belonging, definition of family, and self-understanding were shattered. But my nine-year old-brain failed to give voice to the thoughts that came flooding in. So, we all just went on with our day.

To them, it may have been as simple as their delivery suggested. They loved me, and I was their son. Adoption wasn't talked about much in those days, and having issued the information, we could all just move on.

But it wasn't that simple to me. Not long after my parents delivered the news, I found myself walking down Blueberry Lane alone to get to the school bus and turning the concept of adoption over and over in my mind.

Who puts a kid up for adoption?

How could someone do that?

How could you give up on someone so easily?

What's wrong with me?

Jim Nash and Ricky Farland (my best friends at the time) *weren't put up for adoption, but I was.*

What are my biological mother and father like? What made them have to or want to give me up?

What did I do wrong? I was sure I'd done something to invoke that particular fate.

From that point forward, I lost my footing. I feared I didn't belong—that I wasn't *really* part of the family I'd always known—and I worried that if someone gave me up once, it could happen again. I was sure that with one misstep, I could find myself in a similar situation. I promised myself I'd do everything I could to be perfect so that my parents wouldn't have a reason to let me go.

A few weeks later, I was sitting in that same bean bag chair in the family room. This time, it was dark outside—the first time Dad let me stay up past eight pm. It was the Atlanta Braves' home opener, a night game against the Los Angeles Dodgers. They were playing for a packed house of more than

53,000 people, while millions of others watched from family rooms just like mine. All of us knew that Hank Aaron, a right fielder and one of the best baseball players of all time, could make history that night and break Babe Ruth's home-run record. Some were thrilled at the opportunity to witness a historic moment. Others didn't want a black man breaking a white man's record. Even as a kid, I could pick up on the tension in the air.

It was the second inning. Aaron stepped up to bat. I was impressed by the grace and dignity he showed in the face of so much pressure—which presented for me as a sense of awe. There was just something about him.

Al Dowling, a veteran lefty, was pitching for the Dodgers. Dowling walked Aaron, and the crowd booed loudly.

During the fourth inning, Aaron came up to bat again. The Dodgers were leading 3–1, with Darrell Evans on first base and no outs.

The first pitch went right into the dirt—a ball. The next was a fastball, and Aaron hit it with a satisfying crack. It flew 400 feet over the left-field wall for a home run. At precisely 9:07 p.m.—more than an hour past my bedtime—he had broken Babe Ruth's all-time record of 714 home runs, logging number 715.

The crowd went wild, and so did my dad and I, clapping for Hank at home.

Right then, something clicked for me. I could prove my worth through sports. I was going to become a professional athlete. That night gave me hope—a path to build my self-confidence and show my family I was worth keeping. I loved sports, just like my dad. That's how I could make him proud. That's how I could belong. And that's what I set out to do.

I dreamed about hitting a home run in a big game, lights from the field glinting off the ball as it soared over the fence. I pictured striking a player out to win the World Series, a crowd erupting with a chant of my name.

Those dreams extended to other sports too—hitting the big free throw or last-second shot on the basketball court, or catching a winning touchdown in a full stadium.

* * *

Mr. Hutchinson was my first little league baseball coach. My brother was on the team too, along with Mr. Hutchinson's son, Glenn.

I was so excited to be a part of the team. But at first I sucked. My first season, I only got to play two innings most games—the league's minimum requirement for players. I spent most of my time in right field, where players often found themselves picking the flowers since the ball rarely headed in our direction.

But eventually, I began to pick up the sport and the feeling of community that came with it. On the field, I could also express the feelings I couldn't vocalize at home. I could be angry, aggressive, competitive. At home, I didn't put up a fight. I knew it was my dad's way (the highway or the belt), and so I did as I was told—mowing the lawn and bringing in wood for the wood stove. While I resented some of the ways my parents did things, I was too afraid to speak up—I knew I had been left behind one time, and I didn't want it to happen again. Sports allowed me to get the frustration out of my system.

I could also connect with other kids in a way I couldn't at school. Whereas I worried about messing up in front of them, about showing too much of myself, when I was playing, I didn't have the same fears.

Between my newly discovered identity as an adopted son and aspiring athlete, my paradigm of what it meant to be part of a family shifted as well. Baseball diamonds, basketball courts, football fields, and locker rooms became my second home. Over time, I began to feel like I belonged there, and my coaches and teammates helped build my skills and confidence, allowing me to believe in myself. The way to belong in sports was through performance, and through performance I was rebuilding on my own terms. I wasn't fulfilled personally, yet the feeling of belonging and being valued was powerful. It was a false sense of security, as I would learn later in life, but right then, I was grateful for it.

I also became a student of the sports greats of the day, watching and reading about Roberto Clemente, Muhammad Ali, and Billie Jean King, along with Hank Aaron. And even more than their moves in their respective arenas, I was impressed by the way they stood up for themselves and for others, by how they expressed who they were.

I had read that Clemente said things like, "Any time you have the opportunity to make a difference in the world and you don't, then you are wasting your time on earth," or when Billie Jean King instructed, "Don't let anyone define you. You define yourself." They made me feel like I could push the status quo too—that I could show the people around me that I was just as good as everyone else. I didn't know it at the time, of course, but watching and listening to them helped me become the person I'd turn out to be.

Freshman year High School basketball team

CHAPTER 2

"Courage is fear holding on a minute longer."
—George S. Patton

I don't remember how my parents broke the news that we'd be moving. Back then, I was so focused on staying quiet and hustling to make myself worthy of belonging that my feelings seemed like background noise.

My only goal was survival—I didn't want to be left behind again—and I worried that complaining to anyone, even my family, in any way, shape, or form might put me on shaky ground. Instead, I told myself I just needed to muscle through anything that came up and keep moving forward.

My father had been working in Leominster, a forty-six minute drive from our house in Sturbridge, and finally decided it was time to move the family closer to his job to shorten his commute. I'd start my eighth grade year and my high school career in a new town, Lunenburg, which was about an hour away.

And while I can't recall many details about how it felt to learn we'd be relocating, or even about the move itself, there's one memory my mother, brother, and I share from the trip: My mother got very sick on the ride. That hour-long drive in our tightly packed car stretched much longer as we stopped every so often so she could throw up on the side of the road.

Finally, we pulled up to our new house, a 1,200 square-foot ranch home with a pristine front lawn. The elderly couple who had owned it before us had put in many painstaking hours keeping it perfect (we'd have trouble keeping it up in a matter of months). Inside, my brother and I found our room, a ten by ten space with one closet to share, and a set of bunk beds. It wasn't much to look at, but it would become home.

Fortunately, there was also a basketball hoop outside, and I'd spend the rest of my years there shooting or throwing a baseball against the side of the garage—being careful not to hit the house's siding.

School started soon after without incident, and in my first few weeks there, I found out that the basketball coach—a guy named Turner—was new too, and that he'd be holding tryouts for the eighth-grade team. After all those hours practicing in the driveway, I was sure I was ready. While I so often worried about embodying perfection, I felt confident in my abilities on the court.

When the day came, I thought I did quite well. The other players seemed to think so too, offering me high fives as we made our way off the court and into the locker room.

The team roster was posted later that week, and moments after Coach Turner tacked it up on the wall, we all jostled around it, looking for our names. After a quick scan, I realized I wasn't on it. The others seemed surprised that my name was missing too. A group of them pulled me aside as the group dispersed.

"You were definitely one of the best players out there, Thorney," one said. "I don't understand how you didn't make it."

"Yeah, you gotta be on the team," another added. They reassured me that I belonged out there with them. And while I was scared to rock the boat for fear of being rejected in so many other areas of my life, sports wasn't one of them. I figured that there must be an issue with the coach, not me.

So, when practice rolled around the following week, I showed up and settled into the stands to watch. Coach Turner spotted me out there and ambled up to me as the team warmed up.

"What are you doing here?" he asked.

"You didn't pick me during tryouts," I said. "I'm just trying to understand why."

"What do you mean?" he asked.

"I don't know," I said, grinding the toe of my sneaker into the bleachers. "I feel like I belong on the team. The other players think so too," I said, gesturing at the group below us, a few of whom glanced over every once in a while.

He looked at me for a moment, pursed his lips, then nodded. "Okay," he said, and with that he walked away.

That night, after dinner, the phone rang. I was avoiding my homework when my mom called me up to pick up the phone. I was surprised that it was for me. "Hello?" I said, leaning against the wall and wrapping the cord around my finger, stretching it taught. Coach Turner was on the other end of the line.

"Mike, it's Coach," he said. He cleared his throat. "Listen," he said. "I'm new to the school—to all the kids here. You're new too. And, uh, I realized I made a mistake leaving you off the roster. You're a good player. I'd like you to be on the team." My confidence—and willingness to speak up—had paid off, and that moment served as confirmation that I'd been right all along. I told him I'd be happy to join.

Socially, it was a different story. The neighborhood we had moved to was called Rolling Acres, comprising a circle of around sixty homes filled with families just like mine—parents and kids around the same age. Everyone was friendly, and the local kids would frequently stop by, introduce themselves and invite me to shoot hoops, to participate in clubs, or ride bikes through the neighborhood until the streetlights flicked on and our parents called us in for dinner.

That kind of environment made it almost impossible not to engage with them, but I would only go so far—joining pick-up games and local teams but never taking it a step further to turn those invitations into real friendships. Being vulnerable, letting down my guard, just seemed like an opportunity to prove I wasn't worthy of their attention. What if they found out I wasn't perfect?

For homecoming though, I decided to take a chance, thinking it might be worth the risk. It had been just about two months since we'd moved, and the other eighth graders told me that one of the prettiest girls in my grade was interested in going to the dance with me. They said she was hoping I'd ask her to be my date. So, I gathered up my courage and went for it. She agreed. The plan was to meet at school and walk in together.

That night, I walked to school (it was a short trip through an open field) and waited nervously for her outside the gymnasium, bathed in the music and light that leaked out into the night from a propped-open door. I watched car after car of parents pull up and let out their charges, my classmates spilling out of backseats. None of them were her. Soon, the train of arrivals slowed.

Minutes turned to hours, the last song played, and—just like that—it was all over. She never showed up.

I later heard, but never confirmed, that she was likely drinking with her friends and never made it into the car—an issue that was surely about her rather than me. But it didn't feel that way in the moment. I decided she just wasn't interested, and that it was up to me to learn my lesson. I turned down almost every invitation that came through after that, to hang out after school and go to night games and help build the homecoming float—a big deal in a small town where football was everything.

I overheard my parents discussing me going to visit my cousin Jeff in Maine. They felt that spending time with him might help me open up socially. He was about six years older than me and by far my favorite cousin. They sent me, but the trip didn't change anything. And after accidentally smashing the mini bike my cousin owned into the garage, it was decided that I would head back home.

There were a couple of exceptions when I did accept invitations from my peers. But they never seemed to go well.

Back in the day, roller skating was a big thing, and everyone would head to the local rink on the weekends, pregaming with a couple of beers before heading inside. One rare occasion, I decided to join and slurped down a beer or two in the car before we went in—both to fit in with the other kids and calm my nerves. That ended up being a pretty terrible idea. I'd never had a drink in my life, and I couldn't skate *for* my life. The combination was disastrous.

I tied on my skates on a bench and stumble-stepped my way into the rink, cautiously working my way around its edge. Then, I let go and attempted to push off. A second later, I felt my legs slip out from under me, and I crashed to the ground.

I struggled to get up, flailing as I reached for the safety of the wall, my cheeks stinging even more than my butt. The kids around me laughed as I tried and failed to pull myself up once, twice, then three times. Embarrassed that I had let my guard down and shown weakness, I vowed not to do it again.

Another time, I'd heard from some guys at school that a cheerleader at our school liked me. It seemed to be true. I'd catch her eye as I pulled books from my locker or made my way to class. So, when she invited me over to watch a movie one night, I said yes, pushing away thoughts of that first homecoming dance and how it felt to be left waiting in that parking lot.

Her mother greeted me at the front door. "Mike, it's so nice to meet you! Come on in," she said graciously.

"Hi," I mumbled, offering an awkward wave before stuffing my hands in my pockets and following the cheerleader into the television room.

"I'll grab us some popcorn," the girl offered, as I nodded and settled in on the couch.

I could feel my palms get sweaty the second she returned. I was so nervous. I didn't know what to do with my hands or my face, what to say to her, or how to behave, so I kept my eyes glued to the screen as if it were the most fascinating thing I'd ever seen. Every once in a while, she would try to engage with me, but I stayed statue-still, afraid I'd do something wrong. When the movie ended, I stood up, bid her and her mom goodbye, and left as awkwardly as I'd entered. Unsurprisingly, she didn't ask me back, and I was too embarrassed to ever follow up.

Due to my hesitance to engage, I didn't have a network of friends I could confide in about how the date had gone—if you could call it that. My parents never broached the subject of romantic relationships, and I certainly wasn't one to offer up any insights when it came to my personal life, so I just suffered through it on my own.

Going forward, I turned down any invite that came through, and eventually, they stopped coming. From then on, I didn't go to school dances or even prom. Instead, you could find me out in our driveway, pretending to be Larry Bird or a Red Sox player. It was just me and the sound of a basketball smacking against the pavement, a baseball knocking off the frame of the garage until well after dark.

Sports became my only comfort zone. I was a good athlete for the area— testing my skills not just on the basketball court but in baseball and eventually football, too, and I began to know it. In the locker room, on the field, or in the gym, I could let my guard down a little bit.

Sophomore year, I tried out for the varsity basketball team. Mike Caufield, a senior, played on the team, and his brother, Dave, a freshman, was hoping for a spot. I understood there was some debate among the coaches and some seniors about who should fill the final slot: Dave or me. Ultimately though, the decision was in the hands of the coaches.

A few days after tryouts, I got word that they had decided that I would join varsity, and Dave wouldn't. I hadn't known about any of this ahead of time. I didn't even realize that Mike's brother had been my competition. I'd just looked for my name on the sheet they'd posted when the time came. That is, until I walked into the locker room shortly after and found Mike there, surprised and understandably disappointed that his brother didn't make varsity.

A few days later, when I walked into the locker room to get ready for our first practice, I heard shuffling around the corner. I peeked around a row of lockers. Another teammate, senior Bob Robuccio, was in Mike Caufield's face. "Back off on Mike Thorne," Bob said through clenched teeth. "He's going to be really good, and he's going to help us. Worry about your brother and leave him alone," he repeated. And with that, he let go.

I don't believe either one of them saw me during the interaction. They didn't know I'd overheard the exchange, and soon the room filled with the rest of our team and the creak and clank of metal doors as they got ready to play. It all happened so quickly, and no one had seen it but me.

But Bob's confidence in my abilities gave *me* confidence. I realized someone did care about me. Shortly after, we participated in a high-profile game, and an opportunity presented itself right away. I only got to play for a few minutes—I was new to the team, and only a sophomore after all. But bolstered by Bob's valiant move, I stole a ball at half court and laid it into the hoop with a satisfying swoosh.

At halftime, even Mike was cheering for me. He told me how great it was to have me on the team, patting my back as I walked by. For the first time in a long time, I felt like I belonged.

But rather than focus on the potential connections I'd made, or that I might mean something to the kids on my team, my takeaway was that performance was all that mattered. If you could perform and help the team be successful, everyone would be willing to go to bat for you—nothing else mattered, not race, color, gender, or creed. My heroes—Hank Aaron, Roberto Clemente, Muhammad Ali, and Billie Jean King—had proven that. I decided if I could just do my job and make it happen on the court, I'd be liked for my skill and that would be good enough.

But I remained very reluctant to jump into real friendships, especially outside of sports. *What if it doesn't work out?* I worried, and so I declined their offers time after time. In any other arena, I reverted back to being a loner. Rather than risk making myself vulnerable, I watched, observed, and worked on getting better. Serious and intense, I took on physical challenges whenever they arose, attempting to prove my worth at every turn. Still, I got good at reading people, understanding their motivation—why and how they showed up in a particular way. But I did nothing to put that knowledge to work.

If someone had been able to chip away at the hard exterior I'd worked so hard to create—the way Dorrin would do when I joined Yankee Candle all those years later—maybe it would have been a different story. But I'm not sure anyone knew how.

Teachers and coaches saw a kid with promise, a strong athlete. When they offered help or advice, however, I ignored them. For one thing, I was sure they weren't interested in me specifically—that they were only paying attention or lending their support to protect their own interests, whether that was keeping test scores high or winning the big game.

Adoption had left its hooks in me, but even my parents didn't really understand it and the way it can affect a kid—no one really did back then, and I certainly didn't know how to overcome its impact on my own. So I kept those walls up, as high as they would go.

I was set on being perfect, and if the people I encountered didn't appear perfect to me, I couldn't risk associating with them. For example, my history teacher doubled as the baseball coach. He'd been a hell of an athlete in college at Boston University. But in middle age, he was out of shape. He'd play basketball with us periodically, but he'd be winded and sweaty a few minutes in as he tried to keep up. Weakness-wise, that was evidence enough for me. I wrote him off along with the rest of them, something I'd forever regret.

* * *

More than twenty years later, that baseball coach—the one who played basketball with us every day at lunch—got inducted into the Massachusetts Baseball Hall of Fame. When he got the news, he gave me a call. We hadn't been in touch since I was in high school, but he told me I'd made a mark on him. "You were the first captain I ever had as head coach at Lunenburg High," he said. "I'd like you to be there when they present the award. It'd mean a lot to me."

"Sure," I replied. "Sounds good."

The day came, and I felt the edge of a cold coming on. My throat ached a bit when I swallowed, and the first signs of congestion gathered in my sinuses. I decided not to go to the event. I tried to convince myself I just wasn't feeling well enough to attend. But in reality, I was afraid to see the people I'd known in high school.

What would they think of me?

What would we talk about?

How would I sift through the awkwardness of catching them up on the past two decades of my life?

Those worries crowded out what it could have meant for me to be there—for my coach, for the people I'd known way back when, and for me.

Bob Robuccio, the kid who stuck up for me when Mike Caufield was disappointed that his brother hadn't been picked for the varsity basketball team, had since taken over as head coach of the school's baseball team, and he likely would have been there too. I could have had the chance to thank him for what he did all those years ago, for helping me feel like I belonged.

Then, two months later, I got some bad news: my baseball coach had passed away.

I remember sitting in the church at the funeral, the weight of regret hanging heavy around my shoulders as people shared the mark he had made on them. I thought about the difference he made for me, and the fact that, by choosing to bow out of the event, I'd never be able to return the favor. *I'm never going to do that again*, I told myself.

It took that particular loss to make me realize I couldn't let my fear of perfection—or a lack thereof—keep me from showing up. We all have to choose one pain in our life, regret or discipline. In this situation, I ended up with regret.

[1] "What Was the 'Baby Scoop Era,'" The Baby Scoop Era Research Initiative, http://babyscoopera.com/home/what-was-the-baby-scoop-era/

First week of college picture

CHAPTER 3

"I hear and I forget. I see and I remember. I do and I understand."
—Confucius

"Incomplete." The word was scrawled across the top of my first college paper. I felt my heart sink into my stomach. *What did it mean?* There were no other marks on the loose-leaf, just those glaring red letters.

I'd turned it into Dr. McCarthy, an economics professor and—according to an envelope I'd received during orientation a week prior—my new advisor. He was in his sixties, with a thin line of gray hair ringing his shiny head and a monotone voice. He wore the same dark suits every day, all of which looked like he'd just pulled them out of his laundry basket. Buddies of mine had already dropped his class after the first session, but he was my advisor, so I felt compelled to stay.

I figured it was as good a time as any to introduce myself to him. So, later that day, I knocked on his office door. He waved me in.

"Hi," I told him, "I'm Mike Thorne. I'm in your economics class." He nodded, waiting for me to say more. I held up the paper. "It says incomplete," I said, by way of explanation. "I don't know what that means."

"Well," he said, interlacing his fingers and placing them on the heavy, dark wood of his desk. "I would like you to take another shot at it."

I nodded and told him I'd try again.

About a week later, the next draft I submitted came back again. It had the same inscription across the top. This time, I held it up on my way out of class. "Again?" I asked.

"Again," he said, nodding. "Rewrite it."

A few days after I turned in the third draft, he placed the paper face down on my desk with yet another incomplete. I stuffed it in my bag this time, my anxiety turning to frustration.

That afternoon, I knocked on his office door. "Dr. McCarthy," I said, "I don't understand. This is my third shot. This is the best I can do. I don't know how to make it any better."

"Well, good," he said, "Then I'm actually going to read this one."

"What do you mean?" I asked.

"If you want to be successful," he replied, "you've got to give me your best work first." He went on to tell me a story about how Henry Kissinger had done something similar: He had asked one of his reports for a proposal and made him submit it multiple times after realizing that the first draft didn't hit the mark. Only when the report told him that he didn't know how to improve upon it did Kissinger deign to read it. "I don't have time to get sub-par stuff from someone who I think is very talented," Dr. McCarthy added. "Just do the right thing, right up front."

Dr. McCarthy was old and crotchety and boring. And he was right. In that moment, I began to trust him.

When I did, I started to see that there was more to him than that croaky monotone and rumply looking suits. In class, he'd walk up and down the rows of desks, droning on and on about microeconomic theory. He'd have us read from a painfully dry textbook of the same name. But when I'd drop by his office, I got to glimpse another side of him. There were pictures of his children on his desk. He had a certain warmth to him when he responded to my questions. I could tell he cared about me. That was when my perspective on community—what it was, why it mattered, and my role in it—started to shift.

Picture, for a moment, the family, home, and community you grew up in. Think about what it felt like to interact with your parents, your teachers, your friends at school. You saw them every day, and over the course of your time together, learned exactly how to behave so that you could belong—not just fit in. I came to anticipate the way my parents would react to my presence, the things that made them proud or frustrated or annoyed, and adapt accordingly. The same went for school and sports. Once those environments became familiar, I got comfortable engaging with my classmates and team members in them. But that's the thing: I only saw them in one particular environment. That meant seeing only one side of them, and, in turn, and showing only one side of myself.

In college, those barriers disappeared. Sharing 200 square feet with two or three other people, and a hallway—and bathroom—with twenty or thirty more, everything changed. And that meant I had to change too.

* * *

Move-in day, Assumption University, 1982—my freshman year. I hiked my duffel bag up on my shoulder and surveyed the room. Three mattresses glared at me in all their white plastic glory. Another one had been made up neatly—all crisp flannel and hospital corners. The shelves next to it were stacked with perfectly folded sweaters, organized by color. I dropped my bag on the blank mattress closest to the door. Just then, the guy who the sweaters must've belonged to walked in. "Jim," he said, reaching out to shake my hand as he gave me the once-over.

He asked me where I had gone to high school, what my parents did, and a handful of other questions that felt more like an interrogation than an attempt at getting to know me. I could tell he was unimpressed. My background was no match for the fancy private school life he'd lived up until that point.

When I returned from orientation that night, Jim's bed was naked, almost glowing in the moonlight, the shelves bare. It felt like I'd failed the first test of college. But it was just the beginning of my social-emotional education.

For the first time, I would have a front-row seat to the challenges and issues my roommates, classmates, and teammates had. Without the natural barriers that life in our parents' homes provided, I began to realize that they had many of the same hang-ups and anxieties that I had. And that gave me the opportunity to build confidence in a way I hadn't before. I could make informed choices about who I hung around with based on whether their values were like mine.

It wasn't instant, of course. That first rejection stung and made me feel like I couldn't show too much of myself for fear that I'd be left behind—the same way I'd felt in high school. During the early days of college, I'd head down to the dining hall with the kids on my hall, hesitant to speak up or be choosy about who I spent my time with. While the first communities I built were about proximity—much like the ones I grew up with, comprising family and friends in my neighborhood or on my team—they eventually gave way to ones I composed intentionally. I would come to find the people whose perspectives and beliefs aligned with mine.

* * *

Assumption College (now University) was just half an hour from my house. I'd made the baseball team, and though it was only Division II, since I grew up so close to the college, I'd read about my soon-to-be teammates in the local paper. They seemed like celebrities to me, and that made them pretty intimidating. It didn't help that I showed up to my first practice with a $20 Kmart glove, or that I was wearing sweats, not baseball pants (I didn't own any of the latter).

By that point, I had felt like I belonged on the field for a long time. This felt like new territory. But the coach had worked hard to build a tight-knit culture, and several players came up to introduce themselves, breaking the ice. I'd soon see the benefits of that culture play out firsthand on the field and beyond.

I had a work study job waiting for me on campus. It paid minimum wage: $3.35 an hour and, even worse, it was in the maintenance department. But it was an income, and I was happy to have it. At first, I worked from six to eight o'clock in the morning, before 8:30 classes began. My clean-up duty? The women's freshman dorm restroom. Monday mornings were the worst. I had the awkward task of knocking on the door and waiting for anyone inside to make themselves known. It embarrassed me to no end, and the feeling didn't fade with time—especially when I didn't wait long enough after knocking.

The upside? The two guys who ran the maintenance department. I could tell they cared about me right off the bat. They did their best to make sure I was comfortable when I was under their charge.

They weren't the only ones who had my back. When baseball season started, my coach realized that my work study hours didn't align with our practice schedule and got me moved to the athletic department. There, I worked for the trainer, Brother Paul, a man of the collar. Brother Paul was a cool dude. He called me Thorney like the kids I'd grown up with and the guys on the team, and he treated me like I was somebody—even though I was terrible at taping ankles.

Unlike high school, where I had assumed the coaches and teachers were just reaching out because they had to or because they wanted to have an impact on their own bottom line, I began to believe the members of my new community truly cared for me. I felt as if they were providing the support they felt I needed, rather than offering it as part of some self-serving mission. That support helped me bolster my confidence a little further, even when the going got tough.

It turned out that—as memory serves me—in Division II, you could pick a pinch runner to run for the catcher. On our team, our catcher was All-American player Tommy Westerberg. They wanted to save his legs from time to time and I did have good speed, so if the opportunity was right, I might have a role as a freshman designated runner.

Our first game was against a local college, Clark University. It was a beautiful, crisp New England spring day—a balmy thirty-six degrees, snow showers, with plenty of wind. The ninth inning rolled around, and we were tied one to one. Our head coach was over at third base and yelled across the diamond, "Thorney, get loose, you're pinch running."

I felt my heart slip into my ankles. I'd been huddled on the bench in my coat—it was freezing, and I'd had no expectations to go out on the field. I wasn't ready.

My freshman buddies, however, were thrilled. They cheered me on:

"You got this, Thorney."

"Get loose, you got this."

"This is awesome."

Though it felt anything but awesome, I had no choice. I shrugged off my coat, tried to get loose, and then stepped onto first base. One of our best hitters, and at times a volatile personality, David Riley, was up to bat. He hit a pop fly to right field. Clark's second baseman went out, the outfielder came in, and I began running as I watched it all, thinking, *Oh my God, what if they catch it?*

I decided I'd better get back to first, turning on my heels, my eyes still glued to the ball. Just then, Riley ran by me. Unlike me, he knew it was going to fall in for a hit. He was out automatically.

He was furious, his face turning red, then purplish. "You fuckin' rookie!" he yelled as I finished making my way back to first. I wanted to crawl under a rock. Shortly after, another guy got a hit. I ran full tilt into third base. By then, I was so nervous that I stepped off the bag, oblivious to the circumstances unfolding around me.

Coach yelled at me to get back on the bag before I got tagged out and I scooted my foot back to the base, a cloud of sand coating my pants. I ultimately scored the winning run, but it had been a painful path.

The next day at practice, Coach limped around as he spoke to the team about yesterday's performance, his joints tweaked by gout. "Thorney, yesterday you looked like a kamikaze pilot with no place to land on the base pass. You're done as the pinch runner." My tenure had ended as quickly as it had started—after just one game. I nodded and looked at my hands.

A relief pitcher was sitting next to me, a senior. He leaned over and said, "Listen, Thorney, you got speed. We're going to need you. Don't get down. We got your back. We got you here." I believed him.

Sophomore year, I had the chance to start, and in seeming recognition of the achievement, Coach had upgraded my cheap George Brett Kmart glove to an A2000—Wilson's iconic model. He took me down to Werner's Sporting Goods store.

The glove was bigger and stiffer than my old one; there was no way I could play with it the way it was. One of my classmates, future Red Sox player and scout Ray Fagnant, offered to break it in for me. He certainly saved me the embarrassment of having to figure it out myself, as I had no idea how to break it in.

We went to North Carolina to kick off our season. I also got a chance to bat while we were down there. The first time I stepped up to the plate, I was grateful my baseball pants were so loose; tight ones would have shown just how much I was shaking. After getting behind two strikes, the pitcher threw a fastball right down the middle of the plate. I swung, but it was already in the catcher's mitt when I did. It was as if the ball had to hit the mitt for me to know it was time to swing. Unfortunately, that's not any way to be successful in baseball.

As I slowly walked back to the dugout, I heard Coach quietly call over to our captain Shawn Conrad, from third base, "Go pick Thorney up. Don't let him get down."

As I say today, I am an acquired taste. I'm not not an easy person to deal with, and that was especially true as I was growing as a human being. But they showed up anyway.

People just kept picking me up. They saw something in me. They knew I could do it. And as a result, I didn't want to let them down. I performed up to my potential, because I knew they expected it and I wanted to meet their expectations.

* * *

By junior year, I had settled in. I had the college routine down. I knew the campus, the team, and the guys I'd be rooming with—five of my best friends in a campus townhouse. I knew my academic focus, economics, since I'd chosen it the year prior. Personally and academically, I knew where I was going, and I believed I could get there.

Further, I began to understand the value of the relationships I was building—connections that went beyond the transactional. Those relationships started with a gravitational pull of sorts. For the first time, I began to feel comfortable with the people I met faster than ever before. I had spent so much time trying to prove myself. Now, rather than constantly hustling for my worth, I realized I had people I could lean on. The mountains I'd always imagined having to climb became hills. Their belief in me helped me believe—and trust—in myself. That helped me think about the choices I was making, and do right by my own set of values.

In college in the '80s cocaine was a popular drug. It was in the movies, media, and all over Wall Street—which was booming. It truly felt like everyone was doing it, and those who weren't seemed to be pushed to the wayside. There were a few times when I was tempted "to fit in and try it," but never did. Fortunately, the majority of my friends were not into it. When I felt the pressure to join in closing in on me, they helped me remember who I was, and who I wanted to be.

Eventually, too, I found more friends who had different values than I did—who smoked a lot of pot and drank a lot of alcohol—but didn't have the same expectations of me. They didn't care if I partied with them on a Tuesday. They never judged me for sitting something out. While my other friends wondered why I spent time with them, I saw and appreciated those relationships for what they were worth, and that was enough for me.

Though it would take me years to realize it, my confidence translated to others. People would often drop by my townhouse to chat about life, asking questions I would've never assumed I was equipped to answer, questions about girls or school or what to do after graduation. I responded as honestly as possible, or, when the occasion called for it, just listened.

Many years later, a friend told me, "Mike, you were just the one person I knew I could come to if I needed to talk something through. You gave me perspective without making me feel judged."

Over time, more people began to share similar sentiments about what I meant to them. In 2021, I participated in my first half-Ironman: a 1.2-mile swim, 56-mile bike ride, and 13.2-mile run. When I wrote about it online, the messages came rolling in. One was from a college friend. "Good luck on your Ironman," he wrote. "You continue to inspire me." Another friend said, "You were always our Ironman."

Years earlier, I began to realize that many of us are held back by the lived experiences we've had. We struggle to let go of the past, to adapt to our current circumstances so that we can chase the life we want. People saw me as someone willing to do my own thing, to take a different path to get where I wanted to go.

My willingness to do that may have been due to Carl Ferraro, my first sales manager and mentor at Wilson Sporting Goods. One day, while waiting for my first big meeting, he pulled me aside, "I want you to remember one thing as you grow in your career: You're never going to be liked by everyone. Instead, strive to be respected. Be genuine. Be who you are. People will respect you for that. They may not agree with you or even want to be around you, but they'll respect you."

Having people around me, people who I knew I could trust, who demonstrated that they were willing to help me when challenges arose, gave me the freedom to let go. To accept that not everyone is on the same path, and move forward on my own. And today, I tell my daughters, "When you declare where you're going in life, people will show up in your life."

* * *

College graduation finally rolled around, and I was as ready as anyone to get on with my life. After the ceremony, I was heading back into the gym, pulling off my robe as I went, when Dr. McCarthy tapped me on the shoulder.

"Mike," he said, "got a minute?'

"Yeah," I said, a little exasperated by the interruption.

"I want to share two things with you," he said. "First, I don't want you to ever share with any other Assumption student what you did to get through my classes."

"What do you mean?" I asked.

"You never gave me your best. You waited until the final to show your stuff. That's how you pulled through. I don't want you to teach people how you did it," he laughed.

I smiled. "What's the second thing?" I asked.

"I'm 100 percent sure you are going to have a very successful life. You've got what it takes. And I wish you very, very well. Just make sure you give it your best from the beginning."

With that, he patted me on the back and walked away. He'd been cold as a fish in every class I'd taken with him throughout my four years at Assumption, but he'd shown me support. He'd been a key part of my community, even if I hadn't recognized it until just then. And what he did for me would stick with me for the rest of my life.

Mike and Mag Wedding photo

CHAPTER 4

"Lost time is never found again."
—Benjamin Franklin

I n early spring of 1986, I had a big decision to make: sit out the next baseball season and stay in school for a fifth year to play, or get a job and miss
my senior year of baseball. I had contracted Mono and clearly was not going
to be able to play baseball for a while. I was recovering at home when a high
school friend's dad offered me a job in his insurance company. It seemed easy
enough and would remove the burden of deciding what to do about school
and beyond. Despite that, I chose not to take it.

Brother Paul, our trainer and my boss at Assumption, had a relationship
with a guy named Mike Boylan—an alumni and former All-American basketball player who worked for Wilson Sporting Goods. He suggested I connect with Mike before making up my mind. Mike connected me with the
regional sales manager for the Northeast, Jim Phillips.

The conversation with Jim went well. But I didn't hear anything for a
while after that. Things dragged on through April and early May. Eventually,
during the last few days of senior week and right before graduation, I was
offered a sales job at Wilson with a $26,000 salary—including a car and all
expenses paid. It was a lot of money to me at the time, and I decided to take
it. Plus, it sounded like the coolest job in the world: sports and sales combined. The only downsides were that I had to move and that it would require
travel, two things I'd hoped to avoid when seeking employment.

I'd be living and working in the company's Maryland territory, but my first instruction was to pick up my sales book at the company's regional office in Edison, New Jersey. I had a 1977 Plymouth Volare with no air conditioning and vinyl seats at the time, and I drove it down there from Massachusetts, wearing a clean pair of khakis and my best golf shirt (it was a sporting goods company, after all). I kept the windows open to combat the potential stickiness of the seats so I'd look fresh when I got there.

When I checked in with the receptionist, she told me that my predecessor, Bill Kirchner, was on vacation. I'd be meeting with Carl Ferraro, who would tell me everything I needed to know. In the waiting area, I realized everyone who walked by was wearing a suit. I tucked my sneakered feet underneath my chair as far back as they'd go and straightened the collar of my golf shirt.

A few minutes later, Carl came out to meet me, and I followed him into his office. I took a seat, and he slid my sales book across his desk. "Bill's on his honeymoon," he said. "He'll call you when he gets back, and you'll make arrangements to work together. In the meantime, you should probably find a place to live in Maryland. Oh, and read this training manual."

"How will I know where to live?" I asked.

"Just look at a map and find a convenient location," he said simply. He nodded at me, acknowledging that the conversation was finished. I grabbed the book, thanked him, and got up to leave.

"Oh, Mike," he said, "one more thing. You don't wear a fucking golf shirt to the corporate office. You work for Wilson Sporting Goods and you wear a suit or at least a sport coat and tie when you come here." In that moment, I felt myself deflate. I'd been so proud to get the job, like I'd accomplished something right out of the gate, and before I could even get started I felt as if I didn't belong. And I didn't know it at the time, but Carl would become one of my mentors and best friends.

When I got to Maryland, Bill spent some time showing me the ropes before moving to his new job as sales manager in Chicago, and then I was on my own. Bill was very organized and professional. He treated me very well.

Soon, though, I realized that the buttoned-up image I saw and failed to emulate that first day at Wilson's corporate office didn't quite match the reality of the company's culture. On an early business trip to Atlantic City, New Jersey, I learned that some of my colleagues used the opportunity to get out of the office, away from home, and into drugs and extramarital entanglements. As someone who still prided myself on projecting perfection—and surrounding myself with others who did the same—I was devastated. The trip opened my eyes to the reality of life in this industry.

Of course, not everyone participated in the debauchery taking place. Jack Crabtree and Gene DeCose were veteran salespeople in my area. When things began to get wild at those events, they left. But they were always there to encourage me. I saw the same disparity in our customers. Some seemed pretty slippery, and I hated visiting with them. But because I was paid on commission, my livelihood depended on it. Others were just as kind and willing to support me as Jack and Gene were.

Tony Rugari was one of my biggest customers. His store, Sport Casuals, was in the Alexandria, Virginia area. The first time I went to call on him, he lit into me as soon as I walked through the door.

"Hi," I said, "I'm Mike, from Wilson Sporting..."

"What is this?" he growled, snatching an invoice from the counter and holding it up. "The pricing's all wrong! What the hell is wrong with you?"

I was rendered speechless for a second, taken aback by his reaction and embarrassed that I'd already messed things up somehow. But I was also resilient.

"Let me see if I can get this resolved," I said, reaching for the invoice. As naïve and uncomfortable as I was, I was never afraid to pick up the phone and ask for help.

I took the invoice and stepped outside to find a payphone. From there I called Bill. I knew he knew the territory and the customer, and thus that he was most likely to be able to help me. Fortunately, he answered.

I explained that Tony had started yelling as soon as I walked in, something about the pricing being wrong. "But I checked it twice before I sent it," I explained, looking over the numbers again.

"Well, Mike," he replied, "he's saying the pricing's wrong because you've got to treat Tony differently. He's a VID-two dealer, and you invoiced him at VID-one."

"What's that?" I asked.

Bill laughed. "You don't even know what that is?" I thought back to the three-inch thick sales book sitting on my nightstand, the one Carl had told me to read before starting the job. I'd always been someone who prefers to learn by doing, rather than reading. I'd barely cracked it open; now it seemed like that may have been a mistake. On that call, I came to find out that VID stood for "Very Important Dealer"—somewhat of a crucial oversight. As a VID-two, he was eligible for the best pricing, and I should have been billing Tony at a lower rate.

Okay, I thought to myself, *I can fix this.* I thanked Bill for being so willing to help. He was always willing to help, personally and professionally, and I was very fortunate to have met him so early in my career. He helped shape how I approached business and my customers. I'm forever grateful for his formal and informal training. After our call, I headed back into the store. When I explained my mistake and that I'd be addressing it immediately, Tony softened. I offered my hand, and he shook it.

I realized that it might take some work, and some adjustment on my part—I would indeed have to read that manual—but eventually I'd belong. And with that realization, I started to build some confidence. *Maybe I can do this,* I thought.

That wouldn't be the last time I'd have to consider my approach to customers. Soon after that first call to Tony, I went to visit Howard University, a historically Black university in Washington, DC.

I showed up for my first meeting with Lou Jones, the football team's equipment manager, in a sport coat and tie. I had a Wilson bag filled with samples, shoulder pads, footballs, and uniforms, but I wasn't really prepared. I hadn't done any research on the customer or what he might expect of me.

"I'm looking for Mr. Jones," I said when I arrived and was directed to the locker room. Lou was sitting there with a couple of people, and when he spotted me, he said, "You gotta be the Wilson boy. You got a tie on. What are you doing?" he laughed.

I was still so clueless, and he could tell. Once again, I felt totally out of place. But Lou was charming, funny, and kind, and shared that he was excited to have new Wilson football uniforms for the team. Lou was particularly excited to get them, because the team was going to be on TV for the first time in a while, if I remember correctly.

The uniforms arrived at Howard a few weeks later. After a long day on the road, I came back to a frantic message from Lou on my answering machine.

He'd put the uniforms in the dryer, and they'd shrunk. Now a few key uniforms were entirely too small. Again, I picked up the phone and called Bill.

I started to ramble about the uniforms, sure this was my fault too. "Mike, calm down," Bill instructed. "This can happen." Then, he helped me take the steps to solve it. We would have to order more—ASAP. The first step, though, was to call Lou and tell him the plan.

Once again, Bill was the voice of reason. I was beginning to realize just how much I could learn from him. He seemed to have his personal and professional life down, despite his young age.

Back to Lou... I was pretty nervous that he'd scream at me the way Tony had when I first showed up, but instead he told me he appreciated the call back, and explained where he was coming from.

"You gotta understand," he said, "I got three-hundred-pound linemen who are eating cookies and chips before the games. Their stomachs are going to be hanging out with these uniforms on TV. This ain't going to look good."

I told him we were going to solve it. Then, I rushed an order to a plant in the US, and we got those uniforms redone in time for the team's on-air debut. After they got there, Lou called to thank me and invited me to the next game. "We'll be using your footballs for the first time," he said. "You should come."

I told him I'd be glad to attend.

The night of the game, I arrived by myself and took a seat in the stands. The crowd began to fill in around me. At kickoff, I looked around and realized that I was one of, if not the only, white person there. It was the first time I'd ever gotten perspective on what it must feel like to be the only person like me in a room. That stuck with me.

A number of other feelings welled up, including the feeling that I could do this—and that I could count on the others around me to help get the job done. I wasn't on an island anymore. 95 percent of the people I reached out to were more than willing to lend a hand, solely because they wanted me to be successful.

Around the same time, I was also building a personal community of people I could rely on. One of those people was Maggie Hyland. Maggie and I both went to Assumption College, and I believed she was *the one*.

I remembered her coming to visit our townhouse in college. Back then, she was dating a roommate of mine. As she was leaving I thought, "that is the girl I want to marry" —there was just something about her—though I was far too scared to do anything about it.

Then, during one of my roommate's weddings shortly after graduation, a friend of the bride and Assumption grad Kathy Egan approached me. "I hear you are living in Maryland now," she said.

"Yes," I responded. She mentioned that a former classmate of ours, Maggie Hyland, was living there too and asked if she could give me her contact information. I was stunned that the person I had been so smitten with in school was now living near me. But I played it cool. "Sure," I said, taking down Maggie's number and address. I thanked Kathy, and realized that now I had to make a move.

I attempted to call her, but the number I was given didn't work. Next, I sent her a letter. When I didn't get a response, I decided it wasn't meant to be. But three weeks later, my luck changed. Mutual friends came to visit Maryland, and she called me. We went on a trip to the Inner Harbor with two other couples. As I departed from the car, I invited her to the upcoming Boston Celtics vs. Washington Bullets (now Wizards) game, and she said she had to babysit and couldn't make it. Later that week, she called again and said her plans had changed. The game went into double overtime, and Larry Bird won it for the Celtics. By the end of it, I was sure I wanted to marry this girl. She seemed to be pretty interested in me too, and we started dating. Everything seemed to be clicking into place.

Eighteen months after I started at Wilson, I got some big news. Bill Kirchner, the guy I had replaced in my territory, had chosen to promote me to a key account sales position in Chicago, where he had gone from the Maryland territory. Now he was leading the region, and he wanted me on his team. There were several other young leaders in the Chicago area who likely wanted that promotion, and I sensed they weren't happy about the decision. But Bill told me that I had earned it.

"You know, Mike," he said, "when you first started, I told your bosses that I wasn't sure they hired the right guy, that it might have been a mistake. I'd never met someone so green. But you've proven yourself." I couldn't believe my luck. His style was exactly what I needed, and I was grateful to be working for him.

Plus, how could that kind of endorsement not build my confidence?

Bill went to bat for me too, quickly convincing everyone that I was the right fit for the position. More importantly, he started teaching me how to be a key account salesperson. He was detailed, organized, and disciplined, and he made sure I took on the same traits. I still have the first forecast I ever put together for him. He ripped it to shreds. And then he patiently walked me through the steps of making projections and plans for a business. His guidance served as the foundation for my own success, and he became one of the first people in what became my Personal Trust Community.

I felt confident, too, that Maggie would be ready and willing to move to Chicago with me. But when I told her about the promotion, she wasn't quite as excited as I was. "We haven't even talked about what this could look like, or where I fit into your life," she said. Ultimately, she told me that she wouldn't be moving to Chicago without some kind of commitment from me.

When I thought it over, I was asking for a huge act of devotion on her part, and it was up to me to demonstrate that I would be accountable to her as well. Up until that point, I'd only had to worry about the trajectory of my own life and career. It was the first time I'd have to think about building a life for someone other than myself, and further, about the fact that life was composed of so much more than just transactions. It wasn't just about what other people could do for me, but also about how I could have an impact on them. So I told her I had come up with a plan.

I had been nominated for a sales award, and that meant a free trip to Acapulco, Mexico. Spouses and significant others were invited. I'd propose then. It sounded both convenient *and* romantic.

On the trip, I felt like the ring was burning a hole in my pocket. One evening, when Maggie was standing on the balcony of our room looking out at the water, I grabbed the box and I walked up behind her. I pulled it out of my pocket and cleared my throat. "Well?" I said. I didn't get down on one knee. I didn't have a speech prepared. All I presented her with was a box and that awkward question.

Despite all that—and the fact that she couldn't even call her family because the reception was so bad—she said yes.

Fortunately, my colleagues and their spouses made up for some of my fumbling. After hearing the news of our engagement, they wanted to throw a party for us on the beach! Many of them didn't know me that well, but they were quick to show they cared. That meant a lot to both of us.

In Chicago, we met some great people and began to build a community of friends at the company. Jeff Fiorini and his wife, Lisa, became our best friends. We all have people in our lives who we see every once in a while, but when we come back together, it's as if no time has passed. Jeff and Lisa are those kinds of friends, and I still feel that way all these years later. There were so many others that we enjoyed spending time with, and for the first time, I started to believe in the American Dream.

Bill's willingness to share also showed me that our relationship was about more than just business. He did as much to acclimate me socially as he did professionally, inviting Maggie and me out with him and his wife in Chicago. We grew to be great friends, and I continued to count on him as my family life picked up speed—faster than I could have imagined.

Maggie and I got married in June of 1990. Just a handful of months later, we found out she was pregnant. Having just recently taken over as a key account salesman in Chicago, I was overwhelmed to say the least. Maggie and I had only moved in together after the wedding, cohabitating in a condo in Schaumburg, a northwestern suburb of Chicago. I'd decorated the place on my own and inexplicably chosen to do everything up in blue—the walls, carpeting, you name it. Maggie was making $12,000 per year working at a Catholic school and had about six cents left over from her paycheck at the end of every month. Before she moved into my place, she'd lived in a studio apartment in a "sketchy" part of her town. And now that we were finally getting settled, we had a baby on the way. Everything was about to change again.

That night, I sat on those blue-carpeted steps and wondered how I'd make it all work. *I'm going to be a father,* I thought. *How the hell do I do that?*

I soon learned firsthand that getting to work at seven o'clock in the morning and leaving at six at night just wasn't always possible when there were doctors' appointments to attend and an increasingly pregnant wife at home to support. While the job had to be done, I had obligations bigger than myself and my work. However, understanding that and embodying it were two different stories.

Our daughter, Amanda, was born on May 27, 1991. That night, the NBA playoffs were on TV. A compartmentalizer my whole life, I felt that I had done my job. I'd gotten my wife to the hospital safely, and now it was time for the doctors and nurses to take over. I was transfixed by the game between the hated Pistons and the Jordan-led Bulls, waiting to see this epic battle play out. Meanwhile, I could have been more present, more aware of her needs and what she was going through.

The adjustment following Amanda's birth was rocky for both of us. It took months for Maggie to feel comfortable enough to leave the baby at all—even with me. The first time she left the house to go grocery shopping, Amanda cried for about two hours straight. I did everything I could to quiet her down, rocking, singing, offering her bottles and pacifiers, turning the lights on and off, taking her outside. I was sure I'd never be able to take care of her, especially on my own.

All of us go through new experiences that raise the question of whether or not we belong. Parenting was no different for me. Over time, though, with the right community to help build your confidence—along with the experience only time can bring—you can believe that you are worthy and capable.

A few months later, Maggie and I finally decided we were ready to go out on our own. Some friends had invited us to dinner at a great steakhouse in downtown Chicago. A neighborhood teen had offered to watch Amanda for us, and we felt she was capable. She'd been to the house a couple of times and spent time with Amanda while we were there and had just completed a babysitting course. Even better, her mother was home that night and had offered to pitch in if she needed help. We got dressed for the evening, welcomed the babysitter with a long list of what-to-dos and instructions on how to reach us if necessary, nervously kissed Amanda goodnight and headed out the door.

The drive to the restaurant was about forty minutes, and we were relieved to see our friends when we arrived. It almost felt normal. Not long after the first round of drinks arrived, our waiter came to the table. "Excuse me, Mr. Thorne, there's a phone call for you."

"Ok," I said, following him to a desk by the front door of the restaurant. It was the babysitter. Amanda had been crying since we left. I could feel my blood pressure rise. The sitter wanted to know if I had any suggestions to calm her down. I offered every trick I could think of before heading back to the table.

"Just the sitter," I attempted to reassure everyone. "She's trying to get the baby settled." We ordered dinner, my anxiety increasing as the minutes ticked by. Shortly after my steak hit the table, the waiter returned. "Another call for you, sir," he said, and I followed him. This time, it was the sitter's mother.

"We've done everything we can, but she just can't settle. I'm worried that something's wrong." I headed back to the table, equal parts nervous and defeated.

"I'm so sorry," I told our friends, "we've got to head out." We drove the forty minutes back to our house. Amanda was still sobbing when we arrived. When she saw me over the sitter's shoulder, she immediately reached for me. And within ten seconds of rocking her, she fell asleep—her little head resting on my shoulder, a wet cheek sinking into my shirt. *Maybe I can do this,* I thought.

Recently, Amanda asked me, "Dad, when was the first time you felt you belonged as a parent?" That moment, of being able to provide that calm and comfort, stands out.

* * *

A few years later, things began to change at work. The crazy parties and recreational drug use I first witnessed after joining Wilson started to fall out of favor, and as a result, the raucous behavior that happened at trade shows and beyond just wasn't tolerated the way it used to be. The business landscape was shifting too. Shoe and apparel companies like Reebok and Nike were becoming hyper focused on the consumer. The consumer focus allowed them to grow faster and nimbly move into many categories and with great success. Meanwhile, traditional sporting goods brands were staying the course—paying attention to product and remaining complacent in many ways. I could sense that maintaining the status quo wouldn't be sustainable for the industry.

The company began to go through multiple owners and restructuring, the business plan swinging left and right. No one felt safe. During one Christmas party, a new CEO took the stage. "Welcome to our annual Christmas party," he began. Everyone cheered.

"This is going to be a difficult year," he said. "We've got to dramatically reduce overhead, so we'll be cutting a lot of heads. But ultimately, it'll make the company more successful," he finished. The room was silent; everyone was dumbstruck. How were we supposed to enjoy the party after an announcement like that?

Around that time, the leadership team decided to conduct a sales exercise. Trust seemed to be low both internally and with customers, and the team wanted to get to the bottom of our issues and improve our skills. A consultant came into the room and asked us to identify one thing we wanted out of life. We jotted down our answers and submitted them.

The facilitator began to read the answers out loud. Most people had listed the typical material things: boats, homes, et cetera. Then they got to mine: "I want my F-U money," I had written.

"Who wrote this?" the facilitator asked.

I reluctantly raised my hand. "What's this about?" he asked. I explained that I'd seen several of my colleagues—older men in their fifties who had shown me the ropes—getting laid off or fired. Having spent so long in the same roles at the same company, they were struggling to find new jobs. I was worried I would suffer the same fate. Bill was still in his position, and his supervisor, the VP of sales, showed no sign of leaving either. I figured that, if they were there, I couldn't possibly move ahead. I didn't want to hit fifty and find myself stuck: a one-trick pony out of a job. I didn't want to put in all this effort just to be discarded.

"Nobody at the top understands what's happening, and that makes our jobs difficult. We're the ones facing the customers and saving face while all this turmoil unfolds behind us. Meanwhile, no one's looking out for us. So, my ultimate dream is to have enough money so I can just walk away," I told him.

My father had held the same job at a couple of school systems for decades. His generation believed that if you just put in the time and effort, you'd retire with a healthy pension and some hard-earned free time. But I realized that if I thought I'd just work my way up the ladder at Wilson and find myself in a leadership position thirty years later, I was kidding myself.

I had to start thinking differently about my career. I needed an MBA, or its equivalent, in life.

I soon decided that an MBA would be a waste of money for me. Many, not all, of the MBAs I'd worked with really understood theory and analytics, but their degrees hadn't always helped them work with people. They weren't always great at building relationships, and in my time with the company, I'd learned that relationships—both internal and external—were everything. I'd have to acquire the knowledge I needed through experience.

A company called Franklin Sports was said to be on the cutting edge of customer service and innovation, and when a recruiter called asking me if I'd be interested in working for Franklin—and going back home to Massachusetts—I jumped at the chance. I hadn't been looking, nor was I unhappy with Wilson. I loved my teammates in Chicago that Maggie and I had build inside and outside the company. Wilson's brand was strong as well. Yet something about that call and the opportunity piqued my interest.

And in so many ways, my nine-year-old self was sitting on my shoulder, telling me, "Look out! You are going to be abandoned. You cannot trust what you are being told. It sounds too good to be true. Protect yourself and run." At the time, I didn't understand where my fears were coming from, but each time I felt threatened in some way, my anxiety kicked in and responses were to lash out or, as it was in this case, to run.

I was thrilled to get the job, but one factor made me very nervous: telling Bill. He'd done so much for me personally and professionally. He and his wife had been so kind to Maggie and me. At that point, our lives were entwined. How could I tell him I was leaving, especially when I hadn't even mentioned I'd been looking to go?

It weighed on me, and I wanted to do it face to face. He had meant so much to me in my seven years with the company. The idea of Personal Trust Communities had not yet arrived for me then, but I knew that I trusted Bill and his wife Lisa implicitly.

While I was contemplating how to deliver the news, I got a call from the senior buyer at Target Stores. "I heard you're going to work for Franklin!" he said. "Congratulations! They're going to love having you."

I thanked him, hung up, and stared at the phone. *How did this get public already? I haven't even told Bill yet*, I thought.

I decided I had to track Bill down and do everything I could to deliver the news before someone else did. I dropped by his desk, but he wasn't there. Finally, I called him at home (no one had cell phones back then).

He'd had a doctor's appointment and hadn't come in that day. "What's going on?" he asked.

I took a deep breath. "I'm leaving. I took a job with Franklin."

I could tell Bill was upset, and I could just about guess what he was thinking: *I taught you everything you know, I went to bat for you, and you didn't even have the courtesy to tell me face to face.* But he was professional over the phone. "Alright," he said, after a long pause. "When I get back tomorrow, let's talk about a transition plan."

But after speaking with the VP of sales, Bill told me there was no reason for me to stay. I could pack my things and go. It made sense, of course, I was going to a competitor. There was no reason to keep me there, even for a couple weeks. But it hurt knowing I had let Bill down. Ambition had gotten in the way of an important personal relationship with someone who had gone above and beyond on my behalf, who had stood by me, promoted me, taught me, mentored me, and took care of me in new cities.

When I left Wilson, I was surprised to receive a number of thank you cards.

> *I keep using your name as a reminder of how to get things done properly....*
> *I'll always appreciated the way you conduct business...*
> *There were only a few guys I envisioned being with Wilson forever, and you were one of them...*

The people around me—even the ones I didn't know very well—recognized that I saw the world differently, and that ability had served me and would continue to do so. But the way I handled my parting interaction with Bill lingered in my mind. I'd let him down and put him in a bad position. I'd betrayed his trust. And our relationship would never be the same.

I spent three years at Franklin back in Massachusetts. The Franklin family and my boss, Cliff, were great people to work for. It was such a different atmosphere than Wilson and I learned so much. Being able to make decisions that seemed right for the customers, leveraging all the speed Franklin had to offer to provide customers with the best possible experience, and seeing how a business operates when it is interested in partnering with their customers and not just the bottom line was awesome. It was an MBA in building relationships, all while earning a paycheck and avoiding student loan debt! But then another phone call came in later that would fundamentally change our lives...

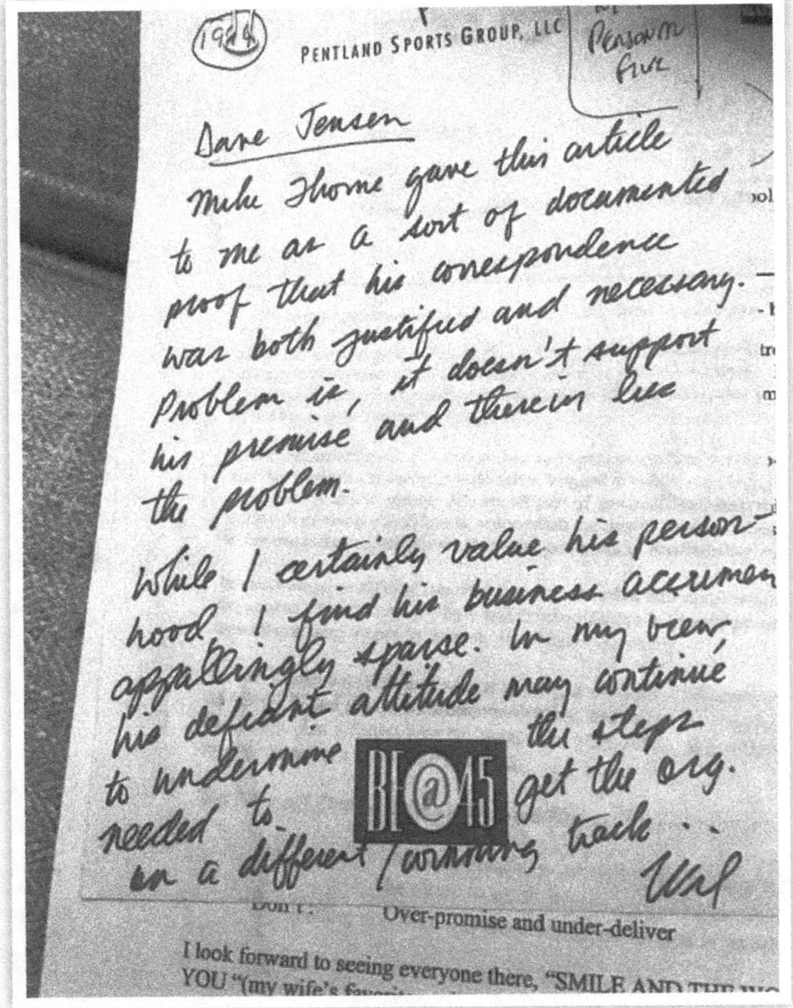
PENTLAND SPORTS GROUP, LLC

Personal
Five

Dave Jensen

Mike Thorne gave this article to me as a sort of documented proof that his correspondence was both justified and necessary. Problem is, it doesn't support his premise and therein lies the problem.

While I certainly value his personhood, I find his business acumen appallingly sparse. In my view, his defiant attitude may continue to undermine the steps needed to get the org. on a different/winning track...

Don't: Over-promise and under-deliver

I look forward to seeing everyone there, "SMILE AND THE WO
YOU "(my wife's favori

A moment of Truth at Pentland Sports

CHAPTER 5

"Things may come to those who wait, but only the things left by those that hustle."
—Abe Lincoln

My phone rang while I was packing up for the day. It was Tony Durano, a search firm CEO. He asked me if I knew of anyone who would be interested in moving to Tennessee to help a European company, Pentland Sports Group, start a US operation. I told him I didn't, but I'd keep the opportunity in mind and let him know.

When I got home that night, Maggie asked me how the day went. When I mentioned that call she looked at me, and said, "I can see on your face that you want to interview for that job." Maggie was always good at reading my mind, and she had good instincts about these things. We talked about it until late, and then agreed to sleep on it.

By the time I woke up, I knew what I wanted to do. I wanted to explore and see where things went. I was young and not sure I had the skills to help run a startup business. Moving to Tennessee also seemed like a stretch, but it couldn't hurt to throw my hat in the ring. I called Tony back a day or two later. Before I knew it, I was interviewing in Tennessee with Joe Fields, who would be the company CEO. I loved Joe Fields when I met him. Army grad, confident yet not outwardly cocky, fearless but not reckless. He was my kind of leader.

Then I got the news that they had decided I wasn't the right person to help run the company, but they liked me enough to set up another conversation with me—this time in Boston.

In Boston, I met with Richard Spanjian, the man who would be my boss if I were to take a role with the company. Then, Joe took Maggie and me out for a glass of wine. Joe was honest about the risks, challenges, and opportunities the job would offer. When he left Maggie and I looked at each other and said, "I like Joe."

And just like that, we were headed to Tennessee. Maggie had moved around a lot as a kid, so she was up for the adventure. Our kids—by then we had three: Amanda, our oldest; Sarah, our middle; and Katie, our youngest—were young enough that we weren't worried about how they'd adapt to a new environment. Instead, we were focused on the excitement of building something from scratch. Tennessee was a lot more affordable than New England, and we spent evenings dreaming about getting a place by a lake, which seemed like a real possibility. I was also looking forward to a new professional environment, the opportunity to get in on the ground floor of an operation and to do it with a great group of people.

We began our sixteen-hour drive to Tennessee, and it wasn't until we reached Davidson County on Interstate 40 that it hit us. A sign loomed above the car as we sped down the highway: east to Knoxville and west to Nashville—we were really moving to the South.

We bought a house in Franklin, Tennessee—a part of Williamson County. The area was freshly booming, due in large part to the fact that a new car company called Saturn had just set up shop there. As a result, Williamson County was among the top ten fastest-growing counties in the United States at the time. What had been a cluster of sleepy farm communities was transforming before our eyes, exploding with new homes and new people. That meant our neighborhood felt very much like the one we had moved from, with folks from all over the country occupying our little cul-de-sac. But we encountered frequent—some subtle, some not so much—reminders that we weren't in the Northeast anymore.

The people we saw around town were very friendly, inquiring about the details of our lives. One of those details was our religion, and they used that information to determine whether or not we were on their team. It made for some pretty awkward interactions, as the Catholicism we'd been brought up with was big in the New England communities where we'd lived, but paled in comparison to Baptist and Protestant religions in Franklin.

"What church do you go to?" people would ask within moments of our meeting, the way others might ask what you do for work or where your kids go to school. Inevitably, they would invite us to attend their house of worship—likely as a generous last-ditch effort to save our souls.

Shortly after we moved, I signed Amanda up for softball. Her first game was about ten miles from home—not too far for a local team to travel. But when we arrived at the field, I realized that driving those ten miles had brought us somewhere very different than where we had been: an extremely rural community. The baseball diamond seemed to materialize out of nowhere, surrounded by acres and acres of crops and the occasional herd of cattle. It looked as if people had left their responsibilities on their respective farms to attend the game, arriving in pickup trucks and dirt-stained overalls. Little did we know, those farmers would become millionaires when they sold their land to the families flooding in from all corners of the country.

My brother-in-law Joe, a big history buff, came to visit the following fall, and told us that Franklin had been the site of one of the Civil War's biggest battles, the 1864 Battle of Franklin. He talked about the bullet holes in a downtown building that served as proof of everything that had gone down all those years ago. He was enjoying his visit.

That weekend, we went to one of the girls' soccer practices and introduced him to the coach. "Joe has been soaking up all the history here," I told the coach. "He saw some bullet holes left over from the Civil War yesterday."

"That wasn't the Civil War," the coach drawled. "It was the War of Northern Aggression. Don't forget it." We quickly apologized and began to back away as he launched into a dissertation about how little Northerners understood about the country's history.

Those cultural differences showed up in the office, too. During one of my first business meetings, I was quite surprised when someone led us in a prayer before getting into the numbers. My boss, Richard Spanjian, caught my questioning eye from across the table and smiled as the guys on either side of me reverently reached for my hands.

For the most part, living in Tennessee was a great experience. We made good friends and went on adventures. We connected with several couples who had children who were the same ages as our daughters and had a lot of fun. We explored New Orleans with other families from our community and bought season tickets to see the newly minted Tennessee Titans play at Vanderbilt, enduring the stadium's metal seats even in hundred-degree weather. So many of the people we met made us feel right at home.

At work, I was excited by the challenge in front of me and was grateful for all the opportunities Joe, Richard and the team gave me to learn. Of course, Joe Fields was our CEO—a young guy with a unique style. He'd come from Proctor and Gamble and Johnston & Murphy shoes, and wanted us to take advantage of some relationships he'd built in Cincinnati. One day, he came into the office and let us know that we would be taking a road trip.

"Alright, boys," he said, "we're going to Cincinnati tomorrow. We'll talk to some P&G people I worked with and discuss where we want to go with the business on our trip."

"Should I book a flight?" I asked.

"No, we're going to take my SUV. We're going to bond on the drive, you, me, and Richard." "Cincinnati has the world's best chili," he finished.

Joe was right, we did bond. It would've been hard not to after spending eight hours round trip in a SUV together. That ride would not only teach me about my colleagues personally and professionally, but also about how to run a business and build relationships myself. The chili wasn't bad either.

Eventually, Joe was promoted to run Speedo, the company's swimwear brand. A guy named Wil Garland took his place. When Will took over, he had a difficult task in front of him. The company was facing some serious financial challenges. In many ways, he had limited choices—all with corresponding pros and cons.

Today, people talk about leaders having both "soft" and "hard" skills, and Will had the hard skills down cold. He was highly intelligent, knew his way around a P&L statement, and—above all—seemed fearless when it came to the challenges ahead and his ability to change the course of the business. In many ways, he was right for what we needed. He had skills I know I—and many others—lacked. That said, the soft skills were not his strong suit.

Despite our style differences, I looked forward to learning some business techniques from him and sharpening my saw, as they say.

Unfortunately, Will systematically dismantled everything that had made working there a great experience, right down to the office's coffee and water machines. If I recall we had been about a $30–$35 million company with forty or so employees. Our culture had been such that you could drop by anyone's office at any time. But amidst all this cost-cutting, Will decided he needed a new office.

Will felt that, as CEO, he needed more privacy and space and built an office that mirrored that thinking. It was a way of exercising the power he had. And it may have been needed in ways that many of us didn't understand. But there is a way to transition a business so that people feel respected and appreciated even as its leadership is making tough choices. Will's approach was to dominate, to make people feel less than and incapable. His expectations became a self-fulfilling prophecy. When you dominate people like he did, they lose the drive to get better. They begin to believe it's not worth the effort.

Morale began to erode, along with our ability to get everyone aligned. Instead of committing to the future Will envisioned, employees became compliant. They were just focused on surviving. The business was changing in so many ways, it became hard to remember what we came to do when Joe hired all of us to join him on this journey.

It wasn't the first time I'd seen Will exercise his power in such a way. Shortly after he took over as CEO, he invited our team to his home. It was a beautiful house. When his wife answered the door, I told her so and thanked her for having us.

"Oh, don't thank me. Will did all of this," she said. "He designed the house, chose all the furniture—everything. I just had to show up." She led us through the house and into the backyard, where Will was sitting poolside, smoking a big cigar and holding court with those who had already arrived.

Will's wife excused herself to take care of the kids, who looked to be about five and seven. She came back out with them an hour later, and asked them to say goodnight to their father. The simple gesture seemed strained, almost like the intimidation we experienced at work extended to their home life. I never asked and had no idea if that was true, but it just felt that way to me.

The leadership team continued to worry about where all this was leading, and how it would allow us to grow and survive going forward. I chose to step in and do something about it. In hindsight, I wish I knew the Rule of Three, a series of questions that can help you make a difficult decision. If something needs to be said/done, ask yourself:

Is this the time?
Am I the right person?
And what should be said?

If I did, I likely would have kept quiet, found a different way to handle things, and not added to my own stress. Instead, I decided to write a letter to Will and copy the senior leadership team. Before I sent it off, I had Joe Fields, the previous CEO, read it. His feedback? "You can send it, but you only do this once in your life." I didn't quite understand what he meant, but I sent it anyway. It was a poor way to deal with the situation and in hindsight, it would have been best to connect with Will and hear where he was coming from. He was a very knowledgeable, intelligent, and tenacious leader who could have taught me so much more.

Will was in Europe on a business trip when it arrived. Shortly after, he called me. "You and I are going to meet at 7:15 tomorrow morning. Your office," he said. "I'm flying back tonight." I was sure I was fired.

I asked Joe what to do. "Just apologize," he said. "Tell him you shouldn't have written the letter, that you should have just talked to him, and that you're sorry. Leave it at that." That made sense. It was time to face the consequences.

Morning came, and I was sweating bullets waiting for Will to arrive at my door. 7:15 came, then 7:16, 7:17, 7:18. At 7:20, my phone rang. "Where the hell are you?" Will barked.

"You told me 7:15, my office..." I said, trailing off.

"I'll be right there," he added. My heart was pounding as I waited for him to come to my office. As soon as he arrived, he closed the door and sat down. He began chewing me out, telling me what a POS I was and how much I didn't understand business.

I followed Joe's advice, calmly telling him I was sorry for what I had done. "Well," he said, "where do we go from here?"

"You're the CEO, not me," I told him. "But I do know that you're a very big fan of Bill Parcells." Parcells was coach of the New York Giants football team at the time. He was known for being a jerk, but he'd won a Super Bowl, so people tolerated his behavior. "Here's the difference," I continued, "Bill won a Super Bowl. You obviously have a challenging job and I respect that. What I don't see as helpful is demeaning the people who work here. And unlike Parcells, we haven't seen any real results. So I don't see how you can continue to behave this way."

Will glared at me across his desk. "Next time, just make sure we chat," he said.

To my amazement, I wasn't fired. But soon after our talk, Will invited me to lunch. He had some news: he was bringing in someone to oversee several of our brands and be my boss—a man named Dave Jensen. Dave and I had worked together previously. "So, what do you think?" Will asked.

"You know, I've worked with Dave before. He and I were colleagues. I respect the decision." But he could tell I wasn't happy with the fact that there'd be another layer of management in place.

A few weeks later, Will invited me to a meeting with Dave in his office. "I'm going to give you a $10,000 bonus for all the great work you're doing," Will told me. "I look forward to what you and Dave will do together."

"I appreciate it, but I don't want the money," I said.

"You're turning down $10,000?" Will asked.

I nodded. "I don't want to be bought. I want to do my job and get paid." As Dave and I were walking back to our offices, he told me he was baffled that I would turn down $10,000. But he hadn't seen what I had, as he'd only been there a short time.

Soon after, we were headed to the big sporting goods show. The night before it started, Dave had put together a team meeting for the staff who would attend. My former boss, Richard Spanjian, and I watched as the scene around us unfolded. The drinks were flowing, and people were getting louder and rowdier. Richard and I decided to call it a night early, exited stage left, and took a cab back to the hotel.

The next morning, my phone rang. It was Richard. "Hey, did you hear? They let Davey boy go."

"My God, what happened?" I asked. Dave was a smart and accomplished leader and fun to be around, so this was disappointing news to say the least.

"Well, he headed to the hotel bar to talk to some Pentland people, but I'm not sure what actually happened." It was another sign that what started out as an exciting and compelling "start up" was turning into a common corporate power struggle. In the process, the culture was being torn apart from the inside out.

The next thing we knew, the company's Britain-based owner's son and daughter, Andy Rubin and Carrie Rubin, were flying into Tennessee for a meeting with us. They announced that they were replacing Will too and apologized for bringing him into the business. He would be replaced with Andrew Leslie, an executive with the Pentland Sports Group organization from Europe.

Carrie Rubin ran the fashion and footwear side of the business, and she met me shortly after the announcement. She pulled me aside. "I have to tell you, my father and I read your letter. You had a lot of fucking balls to write that."

"How did you get it?" I asked, stunned.

"Will's secretary faxed it to my father." I had pushed the status quo, and it had paid off—not just for me, but for the fate of the company and everyone who worked there.

But it didn't feel great, and I often wonder what might have happened if I hadn't written the letter, or if I'd chosen to sit with Will to better understand him and find out how I could be a better resource instead. Not my finest hour for sure.

Shortly after Andrew came on board, he asked me to take on a bigger role and clear out Dave's office to make it mine. While in there, I found a note written in blue marker from Will that I still have today. He was referring to an article that I had left for him and he was not supportive of it. In fact, the last part of his letter says, ***"While I certainly value his personhood I find his business acumen appalling sparse. In my view his defiant attitude may continue to undermine the steps needed to get the org on a different path."*** I decided to keep it to remind me to approach challenging situations differently and be more thoughtful and respectful in handling situations that happened.

I look back and think about how difficult I was to work with and realize today how much stronger from a business knowledge perspective I would have been if I had approached the situation more professionally. It obviously felt like the right thing to do at the time, but as I would learn later on, the question I needed to ask myself before taking action was, *What outcome do I want?* Pushing against the status quo had been my MO throughout my career—my life, even—and it wouldn't be long before it would come back to haunt me.

* * *

I'd bumped up against authority in similar ways before. In junior high, I played baseball in the Babe Ruth League, a boys' baseball program. Our coach was Donnie Barns. We nicknamed him the Vampire, or "Donny Vamp," because of his distinct pallor and the fact that he'd wear his shirt and coat collars up all the time, just like his namesake. He was a very passionate man, and despite the nickname I respected him because he cared so much about ensuring success for all of us.

Our early practices were held indoors at the school gym, and he'd slam ground balls at us so hard, they'd bounce off the walls and hit us in the back of the head if we didn't stop them. His goal, he said, was to toughen us up.

I had decided to play both baseball and basketball that summer, and I began to favor the latter. With limited free time, I wanted to quit Babe Ruth and focus on basketball. Coach Barnes wanted me to keep playing for his team, plain and simple. Eventually, we came to an agreement. I'd play both sports, and if there was ever a conflict, basketball would take precedence.

When I got the schedules, I called Donnie and let him know about a conflict: baseball and basketball games set to happen on the same night. I told him I'd miss his game. He was livid. He told me I wasn't committed enough, that I was disappointing the team, and on and on.

When I got off the phone, my dad asked me what had happened. I told him. "Call him back and tell him you're done. You're not playing for someone like that. I don't want you to be a quitter, but we made an agreement and he's going back on his word. You're going to go get your uniform and tell him to come pick it up. No one's going to treat you like that." And that's what

I did. Coach Barnes came to the house, and I handed him the uniform—end of story.

I learned from my dad that there's a time and a place to adapt, and a time to push the status quo if it means adhering to your core values that few things are as important as treating others well. Sometimes, that meant interrogating his behavior.

When I was in college, my mother was an x-ray technician. One Saturday, she was called into work. My parents held very traditional gender roles and my dad expected her to make his meals. When lunchtime rolled around and she wasn't home yet, he became agitated. I was home on break and I watched as he paced around the kitchen, working himself up.

"Dad," I said, "just make your own lunch. It's not that big of a deal."

"Your mother should be here. She makes lunch every day. She was supposed to be home by now."

"Why do you treat her that way?" I asked.

Unfortunately, he wasn't willing to adapt. He shrugged off my comments, and when she got home, he berated her. She apologized, made his lunch, and continued to suffer in silence.

* * *

When Andrew Leslie came in as Pentland's new leader, he quickly promoted me. But he made it clear that he wanted me to be the eyes and ears of the organization, reporting in to him on what was happening at every level of the business. "Everyone says you're the guy who knows what's going on."

"Andrew, I'm done with that. I don't want to be that guy."

"Look," he said, "I might be here less than nine months. My goal isn't to fix the business in that time; it's to decide whether or not we'll keep funding it. We may be closing up shop."

"Well, I'm going on vacation in early July. If you wouldn't mind sharing with me whether or not you're going to close the business before then, I'd appreciate it." I'd said it half-jokingly, but Andrew agreed. And he held up his part of the bargain.

The Friday before my vacation was to begin, Andrew called me into his office. "Mike, I want you to know that we're going to close the business down. I need you to work with our CFO, David Engel, to put the transition plan in place starting Monday."

I looked at him and almost started to laugh. I couldn't believe this actually was happening.

The next morning, Maggie and I loaded up the kids and set off for North Carolina for our annual vacation with her family, and we began to talk about where the hell we'd go next.

Maggie trusted me to keep us afloat. She'd always been my best friend—still is—and she had faith that we'd figure things out. Plus, between closing out the business and selling off existing inventory, we'd be fine for a while financially. But I worried about what our friends and family would think. They had seen me switch roles every few years, and here I was again, about to upend our lives for the next thing—whatever that was. What would our parents think? Today, making frequent professional moves is typical, but that certainly wasn't the case for their generation, who routinely put their futures in the hands of one employer for twenty or thirty years.

Fortunately, I had a community of people who would understand, people I could count on. Jeff Fiorini, a colleague from Wilson, had become one of my best friends, and he would be there front and center as I transitioned. So would Chris Clawson, who I had met in Chicago back in 1989 when he was a key account person for a fitness company called DP, and we'd connected while sharing space at a True Value hardware store event. Chris and I went out for a drink one night during the show and have been friends ever since.

And our Tennessee neighbors Larry and Julie Nall would help see us through too. Larry would spend hours shooting hoops with me, listening to my concerns, and sharing his ideas about what my professional future could look like.

I also had other business relationships to think about. I had been working closely with Target stores' buyers, and we had just taken over the company's entire soccer program. Our products were set to hit the shelves at the end of September, just a few months away. With the business planning to close down by year end, two whole aisles were at risk of being completely empty. Further, I'd built meaningful relationships with Target's team, especially Melissa, a senior buyer, and Joe Fusaro, her boss. We'd established a Personal Trust Community—a network of close relationships we could rely on when the going got tough. How would I explain to them what was happening? More importantly, how would I fix it? I had to do something to avoid letting them down and leaving them with a financial disaster on their hands. I began working with Andrew and our product teams to buy more time.

Meanwhile, I broke the news to Melissa and Joe using a strategy I still employ today. When I have to have a tough conversation with good customers, I tell them, "Let's take our corporate hats off, trade them for baseball caps, and pretend we're in a bar. There's a beer in front of us." Having set the scene, I deliver the news. Usually, it goes down just a little bit smoother.

I took a deep breath and called Melissa and Joe. "Listen," I told them, "I need you to pretend we're in a bar right now…"

Melissa laughed nervously. I'd provided less-than-stellar news this way before. "Okay, what's going on?" she asked.

They were upset, and reasonably so. We'd spent the past year working on an assortment of products to be carried in stores, and now I was telling her there was a problem. But thanks to our existing connections, we were able to skip some of the awkwardness and fear that comes with hard conversations—particularly among strangers—and start strategizing. Because we'd worked together for a while, building up trust along the way, they knew I wouldn't leave them hanging. "So, what are you going to do?" Melissa asked me.

I told her what I'd done so far to address the situation. She would have to warehouse more product than she wanted to, and in return I offered a combination of terms and discounts to help us find common ground. She gave us the space to think clearly while we gave her the time to figure out an alternative solution, and it worked.

While this was all going on, Joe and Melissa asked me what I was going to do. I mentioned that I was working through my agreement with Pentland and considering my options.

"You need to go work for Spalding," Melissa said. "They brought in these really smart guys from Kraft, but they know nothing about the sporting goods business. They could really use your help."

Less than thirty days later, I got a call from Vaughn Rist, the SVP of HR at Spalding, asking me to send my resume and come for a visit.

They were looking for a Director of Business Development. I went to Spalding's offices for an interview on Friday, and on the following Monday they offered me the job. They wanted me to start right away, but I'd promised Andrew I'd stay on in Tennessee to close things out, and I wasn't about to break my promise. I told the team at Spalding that I would need to start in January if they wanted me to take the role.

When they agreed, I signed on. I wasn't sure if it was the right decision, but it was the one right in front of me. In the moment, that felt like enough.

2005, A member of Russell Athletic Diversity Leadership team.

CHAPTER 6

"I've never let my schooling get in the way of my education."
—Mark Twain

I thought I'd reached the pinnacle of my career.

About three-and-a-half years after I joined Spalding, the sporting goods side of the business was sold to Russell Athletic. After being VP of Sales for Spalding, under Russell ownership I was given what I was sure would be the role of a lifetime—and mine, to be specific: Russell's President of Team Sports. But things wouldn't work out quite the way I imagined.

How did it happen?

Prior to Spalding's sale, numerous brands had expressed their interest in buying the company—Wilson, Rawlings, Adidas, Reebok, Nike—but none of us knew who would come out on top. Everyone at Spalding was nervous about how things would go down, particularly after a disappointing fourth quarter. Eventually, we were told that the sale had fallen through for a number of reasons.

Then, seemingly out of nowhere, Russell Athletic came into the fold.

The business would be split into two, Sporting Goods and Golf, and Russell planned to take Sporting Goods and leave Golf for another buyer—Callaway or TaylorMade. That obviously created a lot of internal anxiety, as people tried to determine whether they would make the cut.

Jim Craigie, the CEO; along with Lou Tursi, the EVP of Sales; and Vaugn Rist, our SVP of HR, were working on much of the transition details with acquirers, and everyone wondered what was being said behind closed doors.

We didn't always see eye to eye, yet I had tremendous respect for both Jim and Lou, as they taught me so much about driving the business and looking for creative solutions to the challenges sales leaders faced. They really elevated my business acumen, and my respect for them as business leaders was very high. Jim had always been respectful of the work I did. He'd even given me a "Never Say Die" award during one of the company's annual awards nights.

One of them asked if I had a preference—sporting goods or golf—and told me that not everyone was going to be given an option. There wasn't a lot of time to decide which way I wanted to go, and there was no guarantee that Russell or Callaway would agree to hire me.

With the deadline in mind, I reached out to the people I thought knew me best and asked them what they thought I should do.

Dan Touhey headed up our sporting goods marketing area. I enjoyed him immensely as a person and respected him as a business leader. He likely wasn't going to be given a choice: it was Sporting Goods or nothing. He and I talked about how cool it would be to work together. Dan also helped me think through the pros and cons of each business and its new owners. It was great to have an objective perspective who could help me think it through.

I asked my college friend Fred Kelley his opinion too. While he knew me well, he didn't really understand the professional implications of such a decision or how it would affect my career trajectory. Still, he offered his opinion based on the information he had and I considered it alongside Dan's.

Maggie weighed in also, of course. But more than anything, she wanted me to make the choice that was best for me.

"What feels right?" she asked. "Where do you think you'd be more comfortable?"

It was an informal—and frankly, immature—approach to gathering advice and insight. The consensus seemed to be Sporting Goods, and when my time was up, that's what I chose.

The team at Russell made me VP of Sales for the Sporting Goods division, placed long-time Spalding CEO Scott Creelman at the helm, and instructed me to grab the best people I'd worked with at Spalding before the golf division got them.

I was concerned that wasn't the right way to go, as I had too much respect for Jim and Lou. Moreover, I wasn't sure that was "right." Scott and Spalding's soon-to-be CFO, Larry Dismukes, assured me that they had spoken to Jim, Lou, and Vaughn, and that they understood and supported this approach. Little did I know what was truly going on behind the scenes. It felt like a game of musical chairs, and you had better hustle before the music stopped.

Sure enough, things got awkward fast. Word got around that I would be recruiting from the existing team, and people began vying for a position in the sporting goods division with the hope that they wouldn't be fired during the transition. It was tricky, considering I couldn't make any official offers just yet. I told Scott that things had gotten uncomfortable—and even a bit ugly— already, but he shrugged it off. He'd handle it, he told me.

Before I knew it, I got word that Scott had been escorted out of the building. Jim and Lou were angry that Scott was taking all of the company's best employees for the sporting goods business. So, they told him he had to build his portion of the business somewhere else.

My office phone rang, and Scott walked me through what happened. He told me I was likely to be kicked out next.

I prepared myself to follow suit. I took a few deep breaths, and looked around my office before packing up everything I'd acquired over the past three-plus years. *This is surreal*, I thought, *How can this be happening?*

I began reflecting on the time I spent and the memories I'd made there, but soon enough, my phone rang again. It was Lou, asking me to come to his office. From the tone of his voice, I knew it was not going to be a congratulatory meeting.

I had walked to Lou's office hundreds of times before, but this felt different. This time, I worried that I'd be chastised and escorted out the door. With that in mind, though his door may have only been 100 feet from mine, I took my time. I circled the cubicles, absorbed my surroundings, and prepared to walk into the end of my time with Spalding. It was like being fired, but not really, because I had a new job.

Because I had such respect for Lou, I was so disappointed that things were ending. I worried about how I could ever thank him for all he did for me.

When I got to his office, the door was locked. I knocked, and waited for what felt like a lifetime for the doorknob to turn.

There was Lou behind his desk to my right, and straight ahead was Vaughn. There was no "Hi," or "Please sit down." They both came at me full barrels about how I went behind their backs after all they did for me at Spalding.

"I can't believe you did this to me!" Lou said. "I thought we had a great relationship." Needless to say, it was a short meeting, and one that—despite trying to clear the air—didn't end well. I was asked to leave the building immediately.

I thanked Lou for everything and tried to explain that I'd been told it all had been discussed beforehand and I didn't realize this was all a surprise. But it fell on deaf ears, and I was escorted out.

While we didn't lose our roles in the new division, we lost our offices in the Spalding building. Scott, CEO Larry Dismukes, and I would have to find another place to build the Sporting Goods business in the short term.

Fortunately, if I remember correctly, Scott had a friend who had some extra space near the local airport. So, we brought our boxes there, and began the next phase of our careers in two small adjacent offices with a broken laptop between the two of us. Now, Spalding—which had been a $65 million business—was part of a $1.5 billion sporting goods behemoth housing numerous smaller brands, from Mossy Oak (a camouflage and outdoor lifestyle company) to Moving Comfort (a sports bra business), and—soon—Brooks running shoes.

There seemed to be challenges afoot when it came to Russell's operations—I'd heard rumors about toxic culture and other issues—but I was happy to be VP of Sales, staying in New England and working with my friends. I also began to build my first intentional Personal Trust Community, starting with a man named Steve Encarnaceo.

Steve was a consultant who came highly recommended by a colleague of mine. He'd worked with brands like Puma and Reebok, and eventually struck out on his own. I wanted him to help me create a team of professional, performance-driven salespeople. I didn't have a big budget at the time—I could afford to pay Steve an annual rate that was about as much as what he typically made in a month. He laughed when I told him what I could offer, but he said he liked me and he liked the work I was asking him to do, so he agreed to sign on.

He was the first person with whom I felt I could really share my fears, concerns, and reservations. He always answered me honestly, and though he usually had strong opinions, he was never judgmental. I didn't feel like I needed to prove myself or earn credibility in his eyes.

"Now that you're VP of Sales, you need to get an assistant to do your expenses, meeting planning—the stuff that chews up your time. The company is paying you to drive growth, and the more time you spend doing that, the better off everyone will be."

I fought it. It seemed petty to have someone else do those things for me.

But Steve stood up, looked me in the eyes, and delivered the message in a way only he could. "Every one of these employees is counting on you to drive sales so they all can feed their families. If you don't, everyone will blame you." Steve was nothing if not direct, but I got it, and he was so right.

With his support, I kept pushing to improve sales, kept things moving, stayed creative, and boosted morale amidst the stress.

It reminded me that when I was working under Jim and Lou, every month, I emailed the senior leadership team to report on our results.

Dear Executive Team,

Another month has passed. This month we had to climb Mount Everest. Good news: we made it. But next time, please make sure to give us shoes—we've got a lot of people with frostbitten toes....
And on it went. It was meant to add some levity and humor to a challenging revenue target.

The story changed with each missive, and kept us entertained as we put in hard work and late hours. I wasn't sure it would be as effective at Spalding, so I tabled it.

A year or so later, Scott Creelman came by my office to let me know that Jon Letzler, Russell's COO, was on the phone and wanted to talk to me. I had spoken with Jon a bit during our regular business reviews, but he'd never called me directly before. Scott went back to his office and transferred the call.

Jon walked me through some corporate changes that were coming and designed to position the company for the future after all of Russell's recent acquisitions. One of those, he told me, was a new role: President of Team Sports.

Historically, Russell had been the superior practice and game apparel leader for team dealers and athletic teams from youth leagues to the pros. The business had been struggling for a few years and Jon; Jack Ward, the CEO and Chairman; and the board agreed there needed to be more focus placed on this division. Then, he said something I'll never forget: "You are the person most qualified for this role."

He told me that I would have an opportunity to be leading what would be the company's most important division and moving to Georgia, where Russell was headquartered, to make it happen. The potential offer came entirely out of left field, and I didn't know what to make of it, but Jon had a talent for putting people at ease and making big moves seem manageable. Still, I wasn't sure I was ready to go to Georgia or take on such a big role. I'd never run a whole division before.

"Jon, I'm flattered, but I'm not interested," I told him. "I don't have any experience running a business," I added, "and my family loves being in New England."

I could hear the smile in his voice when he responded. "I don't think you understand. This isn't really a choice. I've watched you for a year," he told me, "and I believe you have the skills to do it. You've got the leadership and the tenacity we need. Come to Georgia, do an interview, and we'll work it out."

"I've been in sales my whole life. I don't know much about manufacturing, about operations…"

"Don't worry," he said, "We'll teach you."

When I got off the phone with Jon, I sat in the quiet of my office and thought, *Was that for real?*

Selfishly, I was super excited about the idea of running the business, but I was also concerned about moving again and how Maggie and our daughters would see this opportunity. I also wasn't sure how Scott would feel, but when I walked down the hall to talk to him, he had already been briefed. He told me he supported the idea.

I called Maggie right away and explained what had happened. She was nothing but supportive, as always. "This is your dream job," she said.

This is why my wife is my best friend. Obviously, moving to Georgia wasn't ideal, but her response certainly settled my mind down. Although there was an interview process to go through and other steps to take, it was a very likely thing that we would be leaving Connecticut. We decided it was best to talk to the kids that night.

I am not sure I accomplished much the rest of that day. My mind was spinning through all the complications, alongside thoughts about how exciting it would be to interview and see where things went.

On the drive home from work, I thought about what the move might mean for my family overall and how to discuss it with the kids. We had built some great friendships in our neighborhood and town. We'd just finished building a sun porch in the back of our house and had been looking into putting a pool in the backyard. When it came to living there, we were "all in."

Meanwhile, if I got the job, we would have to move to Georgia—something none of us had on our "bucket list" of things to do. That night, we held a family meeting in the living room, and I told the kids about what I'd been offered. Our oldest, Amanda, was in eighth grade. We'd been in our home for three years by then, and she didn't want to be uprooted again. I can still see her shaking her head at me from her perch on the arm of the couch.

Soon after, when I flew down to Georgia for the interviews, I told Russell's SVP of HR, Ed Flowers, that I didn't want to move. "My family is number one," I said. "If things don't work out, I need to be taken care of."

"Don't worry," he replied dismissively, "we'll take care of you." In hindsight, I should have asked a few more questions.

"What do you expect to get paid to do this job?" he asked.

Fortunately, before the meeting—unsure of how much they would offer—I reached out to Joe Fields, whom I'd worked with in Tennessee a few years earlier and whom I trusted. He told me to calculate 35 percent more than I was making as VP of Sales as a starting point, and said he'd be a reference if Russell needed one.

It would be a big change, but this was what I had been working for. When they made me an offer, I accepted.

Before I left, the team at Spalding threw me a small going-away party, and gave me a basketball they all signed. I certainly felt appreciated, but looking back, I wasn't as gracious or grateful as I could have been.

In truth, I wasn't mature enough to reflect on my time there, thank everyone who had helped me on my journey, and take those lessons with me—and I paid for it as a result. Sometimes, pausing and "debriefing" to ensure you capture the lessons learned and the memories made is essential for growth. But I saw the new role as the next phase of my journey and the natural progression in my career and just forged ahead. I recommended a replacement for my role to Scott, and then I prepared to move on.

We put our house on the market and sold it in three days. My family and I were in Georgia in two months, even faster than any of us expected—the team at Russell included. As promised, Russell did send me to get formal training to learn the ins and outs of being a president. I ended up parallel pathing, working on the business while attending a special three-week executive education program at the University of Pennsylvania's Wharton School of Business in Philadelphia.

It was awesome to be around highly accomplished senior executives from around the world and I regret not staying in touch with them. Most of the courses consisted of intense "training," alongside a lot of casework and scenario planning. It was fascinating, but looking back, I would have received more value by working on the business for a stretch of time before taking the course. I would have had more context if I had waited, but I was so focused on handling the task at hand and taking on the job I was being asked to do.

Going in, I was quietly confident. I saw it as an opportunity to take the reins and do what I thought was right with a very experienced group of people. That is, until Jon sent a note out about a company meeting, and shared the first order of business: I would be introducing myself. I immediately went into fear mode. That nine-year-old kid was back on my shoulder, telling me to run away. I closed the door to my office and began pacing the floor.

How am I going to get up in front of these people?
What the hell am I going to say?
Who am I?

I decided to call Steve. I told him everything I was feeling—how scared I was, that I was worried I didn't belong. "Maybe this isn't a good idea," I finished.

"Mike, business is a show. You've got this. The industry is looking for Russell to lead, and you can be that leader. Every good speech has a simple three-part framework," he said, laying it out for me. Over the next few days, he continued to coach me on what to say and how to say it.

I got through that call, and then things became really real. People began showing up at my door with all of the company's problems, looking to me to solve them. They shared them in meetings and on walk-and-talks. And the more I listened, the more I realized how daunting the issues really were. This was going to be even more than I bargained for.

In one meeting, I was hit with the full weight of it. Successfully managing the manufacturing plants would be critical to my success, and that of the company, including plants in Mexico and Alabama.

In addition, Russell had just bought a brand called BIKE Athletic, which made football helmets and other protective gear, as well as apparel. It was explained to me that BIKE would be exiting their apparel business. The Russell strategy was a "head to toe" solutions model for athletes. Russell would remain the apparel solution, BIKE would cover the advanced protective equipment, and Spalding would provide the sports equipment. It made sense on a piece of paper for sure. But, as I was to learn throughout my career, when you insert people into logic without thinking through the realities of execution, things can get complicated. And I was about to learn it the hard way.

I had met the BIKE leadership team prior to our monthly financial review. I loved their passion, and I could tell they felt like no one respected them. I distinctly remember how they passionately recounted BIKE's history as the inventor of the jockstrap, the product's biggest seller to date. It was as amusing as it was informative. So, when I was asked if I wanted to run BIKE as well, I said yes.

But when it came time for BIKE's first financial review, I didn't have any of the data. "Don't worry," one of BIKE's leaders told me, "our CFO always takes care of that. He is on board with the equipment strategy."

Three hours later, I found myself in a room of up to twenty people, including Jack Ward, Russell's CEO and chairman, waiting for the review to begin. The CFO began running through the numbers. "We've gotten rid of about $200,000 in apparel," he said.

"Sorry?" said Jack.

"We've gotten rid of $200,000 in apparel," the CFO repeated.

"What the hell are we getting rid of the apparel for?"

I spoke up, thinking it was my job to be the answer person. "As you know, we're launching advanced athletic protection for BIKE. We removed the apparel because Russell's taking it on."

Jack went off. "That's not why we bought this brand!" he yelled, launching into a tirade.

I turned and looked around the room to all the leaders who were well aware of the plan. I even asked the former BIKE leader, Rod, to speak up. "Can you just walk through the advanced athletic protection strategy?" I requested.

Crickets. He didn't say a thing. No one else did either. The room was completely silent, and I was left hanging—the product of a culture where no one felt comfortable enough to speak up. It was a sight to see senior executives, all of whom were bright and accomplished, freeze because they were afraid to communicate honestly.

I walked out of that meeting feeling small and frustrated, and over time that frustration only grew. Unfortunately, I wasn't great at hiding it.

I found myself expressing myself by venting and cursing in meetings, unable to shoulder the stress. I started to doubt that I was up for the job.

The same insecurities I'd been grappling with since I was a kid—that maybe I didn't belong in my role, or at the company—showed up once again. And the more I felt like I didn't belong, the harder it was to control my emotions. Just as I had when I was nine, I feared that I'd be abandoned, left behind for doing the wrong thing. I started questioning everyone's motives and even worried about trusting the people around me, sure that they would jump ship or throw me under the bus whenever they got the chance. Ultimately, it would become a self-fulfilling prophecy.

Before I joined the company, Russell had hired a McKinsey consultant who I was told was costing the company something like $1 million per year.

He had been working on several aspects of the business overall. I sat in on one meeting with him related to the Team Sports division, and I could tell right away that his ideas about the team sports division were not resonating. As a result, he had been unable to gain traction on much of his agenda. He was focused on the business, and people wanted him to meet them where they were instead. I didn't see us executing on his suggestions, so I told him we wouldn't be needing his services anymore in the team division.

Shortly after my decision, I got an earful, along with the reminder that it was on me to fix the business. While it was my choice, the results were on my shoulders too. I'd have 90 days to put together a plan to make things work and present it to Jack and Jon.

Our team had a lot on their plate already. But I was so grateful to all of them for the way they stepped up and helped assess the business challenges, as well as solutions. Ultimately, though, I knew that it would all come down to execution.

I decided to bring in Steve, the consultant who had become a key part of my trust community. And I'd pay him $60,000 a year to be Russell's consultant, rather than a million. Steve and I worked to come up with those solutions, collaborating with the team and building a plan to make things work. But our issues continued. We were having problems with our product.

As Steve and I dove in deeper, we began to see that at the root of our struggles was that we lacked a cohesive communication plan across the company. For example, Russell had hired someone to help the business transition away from being a full domestic manufacturer and explore an import strategy. It seemed to make tremendous sense, as it would save money and open us up to new ideas. But we ran into issues with execution.

Unfortunately, there were differences in the color of the apparel manufactured at Russell's factories in the US, and those we imported. The end result was a series of mixed inventories on the same stock numbers. Individual teams were getting gear that didn't match. Those inconsistent colors meant millions of dollars of unusable inventory—just one of many conundrums plaguing the business.

As the ninety-day mark neared its end, I remember Jack or Jon letting me know that they were hiring a new CEO to oversee all of Russell Athletic, and

I'd be reporting to him. "His name's Calvin," Jack told me. "He's going to be great. You'll like him."

Now, I am sure I may have met Calvin during a few of the quarterly reviews. I believe he was running a small piece of Russell's business in Europe at the time. But he had never run a company like this before, and, during one of my first meetings with him, he wanted an overview of the work we were doing and how things were going. I explained my role, our team's plan to fix the business, and the fact that Jack and Jon had asked for a plan in the first ninety days, which was coming up.

"We're not doing that," he said simply. "We don't need to meet with Jack to fix this business, I'm going to fix it. Cancel the meeting. Jack and I are good friends, and I'll handle this with him."

Once again, I didn't do much to hide my frustration. When I was done meeting with Calvin, I went to Jon. I explained that the team had put hours and hours into the plan, that I thought we could fix the business with it.

"Ok, let me handle it." he said.

Jon talked to Jack, and told me I could make my presentation.

The day came to present, and I was feeling confident once again. Our team, especially our head of marketing John Sabol, did an amazing job. I was so grateful to everyone for pulling together to help make the story work well. I'd gone to bat for my team, and we were given an opportunity to make our case.

Things seemed to go quite well. We laid out the financials, walked through the issues we'd uncovered, and shared our plan to get the business back on track over a three-year period. I remember Jack looking around the room at all the samples we had set out showing the color issues, the quality challenges, and then turning back to the bleak short-term financials. "How the fuck did this business get so screwed up?" he said, shaking his head. Despite that, he agreed to what we'd proposed, giving us the green light to take action.

Soon, Jon was less involved with our business (he would even leave the company at some point over the next several months), and Calvin showed up at my office door. He sat down across from me.

"We're not doing it the way you want to do it," Calvin said, steepling his fingers. He told me *his* plan: to focus more on the private label opportunities that existed within Russell Athletic as a brand overall. I could see where that might end up.

"Calvin, we are selling t-shirts to college and pro teams at great margins, and I don't see how selling more "private label" will help this business financially. I cited all the reasons it wouldn't work, including the manufacturing variances that had already created issues for us. "If you're going to do that, you don't need a President of Team Sports," I said angrily. "All you need is a sales guy."

Two months later, on December 21, 2005, he called me into his office. "Mike, I'm eliminating the President of Team Sports position. Please go see HR to sort things out."

Once again, I was facing the end of a role with plans to head out on vacation. My family and I were going to Disney World in just a few days.

"Hold on a second, Calvin. I didn't want to take this job. I didn't want to move my family to Georgia. We have worked so hard to rebuild this business over the last year. And now you're telling me that you're eliminating my role? They said they'd take care of me—take care of my family."

"I wasn't here when they told you that," he said, nodding at the door. Now in Calvin's defense I drove him crazy during his short time there, expressing frustration with the lack of action on key issues. He had a lot on his plate and my business was a small portion of what he was dealing with.

Time seemed to slow as I walked to HR and visited with Ed Flowers, a senior executive and someone I had great respect for. I asked about what they had promised me. "Sorry, there's nothing we can do. Calvin made the decision. He's the boss. Jack supports him."

I was angry. They'd broken their promise, and I was about to have to tell my family that our future was up in the air yet again. I'd gotten close with Jim Evans, the VP of HR, and before I walked out, I stopped by his office.

"Mike, you did a great job," he told me. "This place will be devastated when you leave. People really thought you were the one person who could fix it. Think of it this way: We were all sitting around a boxing ring, and you were in the center. But rather than a person, you were up against the culture—a formidable opponent.

"We were all waiting to see if you could take it on and change it. But no one stepped into the ring with you. They wanted to see if you could be successful before they came to support you. It's not all your fault."

It was around one o'clock in the afternoon when I finished talking to Jim. I called Maggie from the office in complete disbelief. It took me a minute to gather my thoughts enough to tell her. I felt horrible. Then, I drove home, the sun still high in the sky.

The girls would be home from school in just a couple of hours, and I would have to break the news to them and everyone else. We'd only been in Georgia for fourteen months. *How the hell am I going to tell people I just got fired?* I thought. Just over a year ago, I had told our friends and family how amazing this role was going to be.

My confidence had been shaken. I many ways, my fear that I didn't belong had been realized. I began to wonder if I shouldn't have been president in the first place. *Maybe I wasn't qualified to run a company. Maybe I didn't belong in the C-suite. Maybe I am just a sales guy. Or maybe I should quit this stuff altogether and become a coach.*

I'd set up a basketball court in our driveway, and I grabbed a ball from the garage and started shooting baskets by myself. I was furious, but more than anything, I was humiliated.

Years later, my kids would tell me they knew something was wrong as soon as they stepped off the bus and saw me out there, taking shot after shot.

Maggie was frustrated and angry—reasonably so. We had uprooted our family to make the move, and fourteen months in, we had to figure out our lives once again. She was demoralized, frustrated, embarrassed, and she wanted answers. But I couldn't point to what I'd done wrong, exactly. They'd eliminated the position, Calvin said, and I'd never know whether they had done that because of me, or because they truly didn't need someone to run things at that level.

For a while, I was mad at the world. I couldn't see that, regardless of what they'd said, I'd had a hand in the outcome myself. That—while we pulled together a plan that could've been effective—I made a lot of missteps along the way. I hadn't always acted like a company president, and for that, I paid the price. I was so focused on fixing the business that I forgot about the human side of things.

First, I reached out to the people who I knew would say what I wanted to hear. They told me just that. The company had made a mistake, they didn't know what they were doing, my old colleagues would help me figure something out, and more. But I soon realized that didn't really help the situation. It was a balm for my bruised ego, but little else.

I had been promoted from one position to the next throughout my career, and I'd figured that if I'd been getting job after job, I must have been doing everything right. When Russell, a very prominent company, decided to put me at the helm of the most important business they had, I figured I must be good. And rather than see the individuals around me as confidants who could provide important insight on how I could get better, I saw them as people who would come on the journey with me, and support the efforts I thought were necessary. More than anything, I cared about being perceived as perfect, just as I had as a kid. Sporting goods was all I knew, and that's why I had chosen it. I thought that there would be less room for error that way.

Moreover, I didn't know how to be vulnerable enough, to share what I was struggling with and get the feedback I needed to make better decisions and grow personally and professionally.

Eventually, I realized that I'd played a role in my own undoing, and I wanted answers. Further, I came to recognize that, outside of I love you, the three most powerful words you can utter are "I need help."

It was the first time I ever got punched that hard and didn't see a way out. I didn't know how I'd get out of it and into the next thing. I couldn't see a clear path to recovery.

But by then, I'd built a trusted community of people I had a lot of faith in and who had a lot of faith in me in return. I thought they might be able to help me work my way through it. So, I reached out to some of the people I'd worked with at Russell, Spalding, and friends I had met throughout my career. I asked for help in the form of feedback and perspective, and they answered honestly.

Several leaders who I reached out to gave some insight that was particularly hard to hear, but it was the perspective I needed. Many essentially said my self-awareness sucked. In fact, it was non-existent. "Your self-awareness and your emotional intelligence were nowhere near where it needs to be for a person running a business," several people told me.

Scott Creelman, who was the President at Spalding, and Larry Dismukes, the CFO at Russell, provided similar feedback. They told me that we had good ideas and I had the IQ and the drive to make it work. But the emotional intelligence just wasn't there. I got too frustrated, too distracted. They told me that it was obvious that I was overwhelmed, not just from what I said, but from what I did—the way I held my body. I asked my consultant Steve why he thought things went south. While he thought I'd been around a bunch of idiots, he'd also seen limitations in the way I carried myself.

I wasn't ready for quite so much honesty. While I'd wanted to know what went wrong, I was hoping for more empathy than I got. That said, it seemed to have a little cushion to it. It didn't hurt nearly as bad as I thought it would. And I realized they were right. I'd learned firsthand that getting frustrated and showing it just didn't cut it. All I succeeded in doing was transferring my stress to the rest of the organization. That realization paved the way for the biggest professional transformation I would have to date.

There was good stuff too. People wrote to tell me that I had brought the team together, that they couldn't believe this had happened to someone who really cared about the people. Meanwhile, no one ever—in any job I've ever had—wrote to tell me that I did a great job hitting the quarterly numbers. They wrote that they'd miss my teaching, the way I trained and developed them. They told me I was the only person who cared about people, that I got in the trenches with them. That was what stood out to them. And those insights hit me like a two-by-four across the head—but in a good way.

I was in a lot of pain, but we decided to take our Disney trip anyway. It gave me the space to remember what really matters in life.

The kids gave me a hard time. "Dad, you're still fired, right?" they'd ask. "But you're still gonna go on this ride…" Their jokes helped me realize that, to them, I was still the same dad I'd always been. They didn't abandon me.

And as I processed my colleagues' feedback in the weeks that followed, I began to realize that life isn't a straight line. What had happened to me happens to everyone in one way or another.

Of course, I had some things to figure out when it came to the next step on my path. My wife and I had promised the kids we wouldn't move somewhere new, and that meant we had to stay in Atlanta or move back to Simsbury, Connecticut, where they'd spent most of their childhood.

I also wanted another chance to work with a great group of people, be part of an organization, and hopefully run a business. There were a limited number of sporting goods companies in Atlanta. Mizuno was there, but it seemed to be struggling and it was driven from Japan. And candidly, my family didn't want to live in Georgia anymore. Everyone wanted out, and I couldn't blame them.

Change was afoot in the industry too. When I left, the same companies that had always dominated the space—old-school businesses like Russell, Champion, BIKE, Spalding, Wilson, and Rawlings—still ran the scene. They each did their own thing, with no one interested in disrupting that "model." But Nike and Under Armour were starting to expand their brands. Nike was branching out beyond footwear and apparel. And Under Armour was just beginning to become a behemoth that other brands didn't take seriously enough. They were putting a lot of pressure on the old guard. The thing is, the old guard was unwilling to confront the reality that these brands were going to dominate the sporting goods industry going forward. Despite this threat, the old-school businesses just kept plodding along.

Russell felt very manufactured: everything came down a chain of command. Everyone had embodied the message that all of us were just there to get things done—cogs in the wheel of a manufacturing machine. The people who did the "real" work, those who dealt with customers and heard the cries for change, were not listened to. Much of the leadership team, all talented and very equipped to come up with the ideas necessary to compete in an evolving landscape, spent more time politicking or positioning themselves well than actually pulling people together. We were very process-driven—focused on what we did and brought to the marketplace. It was about us, rather than the consumer.

That's what Nike, Under Armour, and others changed. They kept their assets light, so they could listen to the consumer and adapt. And rather than housing tons of product in big warehouses like we did, they sourced many of their materials from Asia.

Those factors were playing in my head as I considered our family's next move. I weighed potential opportunities at Nike in Portland, Oregon, and

Adidas in California, but Maggie and I weren't interested in moving to the west coast.

As I thought about all of this, I had even big questions to ponder. Who did I want to be as a leader, what did I learn from this experience, what could I take advantage of as I transitioned, and how would I transform again? Most importantly, what role did I play in the demise and how to avoid it happening again.

Dear Santa,
Merry Christmas! I have a couple questions for you! Answer the best you can!

special (or is it natural?)
• Is there anyway to make reindeer fly?
• How long have you lived?
• What's your history?
• Which title do you prefer?

Love,
Sarah.
• St. Nicholaus?
• Santa Claus?
• Chris Cringle?

P.S. Write Back on the back!

Sarah,
  Santa is who you believe and can be called any of the names you asked.
  I live forever in the North Pole.
  Do you know that Santa loves you and all the children in the world?
      Love
      Santa

Dear Dad,

You're always there for me and our family. You've never doubted my abilities and you've taught me everything that I know today. Because of you I've been raised the best way any kid can ask for.

Dad spending time with my daughters

CHAPTER 7

"I don't care what you feel. I care what you're committed to. I'm speaking to your dreams."
—Bo Eason

After more than twenty years in sporting goods, I'd seen the good, the bad, and the ugly. Now I was facing down the fear I'd had when I first started at Wilson, that I'd be fired after a long career, unsure of how to make it in any other field.

At age twenty-five, I decided to forgo an MBA and instead pursue an informal business education, with a concentration in life skills. And in 2006—at age 40—I was straddling two worlds: the one in which my parents lived, where it was common to work for the same company for four decades, and the one in which my children would work, where the average American changes jobs every four years.

Moving around as frequently as I had wasn't that common, though times were changing, and I could feel it. But with the sporting goods companies that were pushing the envelope, like Nike and Adidas, both based out West—somewhere Maggie and I weren't interested in moving—I wasn't sure what to do next. Under Armour was on the move and sensed it would disrupt the industry even further, but its offices were in Baltimore, Maryland, yet another place we weren't sure we wanted to go if something materialized.

I worried that, outside of these industry disruptors, sporting goods companies had become entirely complacent, holding fast to the status quo. I didn't want to go to a business that wouldn't be at the forefront of progress. Meanwhile, I wasn't sure how *I'd* progress, particularly with the seemingly limited skill-set I'd built over the course of my career. I was beginning to realize that I needed to build my personal and professional tool box once again. And then my phone rang.

It was toward the end of January when Spalding called me. They asked me if I'd consider coming back. They were planning to ramp up their baseball glove department, which was run by a licensee. The CEO of that licensee was a former boss of mine and someone who remains in my Personal Trust Community today, Carl Ferraro. There was a potential for me to move back to Simsbury, where our kids had spent most of their school lives, and run the license from there. I would commute periodically to New York where the licensee headquarters were. It would be a chance to develop and grow a business, and on the surface, that sounded great. Hearing from the company where I still had friends served as a bit of a confidence boost. The role would involve things I hadn't really done before, so I didn't quite believe I could do it, but I was interested in the opportunity.

Soon after, a financial services company, Gerson Lehrman Group, reached out. They asked if I'd be interested in coming to New York to meet with a group of hedge fund people. They would bring me in for lunch, and pay me $1,500 for an hour of my insights. All I had to do was answer some questions about the current state of the apparel industry and—more specifically—what I thought about the future of Under Armour and its role in the industry versus Nike and Adidas.

That call alone gave me some confidence. They'd reached out to me because of my experience and knowledge. It was a reminder that I knew what I was talking about. But on the flight to New York, and in the cab to their offices, that confidence started to wane.

I met an executive in the building's lobby, and as we walked to a nearby restaurant, my palms began to sweat. Maybe I didn't know as much as I thought I did. Ten men were gathered around a big circular table, all dressed identically: black sport coat, white shirt, and tie. They looked exactly as you'd imagine a group of hedge fund guys to look—young, ambitious, analytical.

The moment I sat down, they launched into a million questions about if, how, when, and why Under Armour would get crushed. I shared my point of view, and challenged them on their thinking, telling them why I thought the company would thrive. How they were creating an entirely new segment of apparel and how others didn't take them seriously enough. It was my belief that these hedge fund people were missing the point of what was happening. An hour later—as promised—they were done.

I had no idea whether it went well or not; no one said thank you. But the man who had walked me in also led me out. "You did a great job," he said. "I think they got a lot out of it." His words gave me a glimmer of hope that I could find myself back into a C-suite role someday.

Then, another call came through. This one went to voicemail—but it would change my trajectory entirely. It was from a man named Drew Braiser. His daughter and mine were friends. We didn't know each other very well, but he'd heard I was looking for work, and he had an opportunity for me, if I was interested.

"Yankee Candle's looking for a president. A search firm contacted me about the position. I'm not interested in the role, but I'll connect you, if you'd like," he said.

I was nervous about the potential of entering entirely new territory, but I was definitely interested. I began researching. What I saw was a high-end performance brand. But more than that, Yankee Candle appeared to be a people-focused company committed to understanding and serving its customers. Home fragrance is personal by nature, after all. I figured that kind of environment could teach me a lot, all while aligning with what I believed was the right way to run a business: You've got to hit financial targets, but you also have to care about the people.

The company was public at the time, which also intrigued me. The position appeared to be open due to a desire to "reimagine" the wholesale business—that's why they were looking to hire in the first place—but what stood out to me were the positives: a people-centric mission and vision in a people-centric industry. The culture seemed to be everything I'd ever dreamed of. And while I'm not religious, I'm spiritual enough to believe that there might be a reason I had been looped into this opportunity seemingly out of nowhere. *Maybe this could be my next growth opportunity*, I thought, and decided I had to pursue it.

Maggie would have preferred that I go after the Spalding role—it seemed safer, and it would have allowed us to live the life we'd had before. But I was ready for something different, and this was my chance.

The first interview with the search firm didn't get off to a very good start. They had scheduled me for a video call, but I wasn't sure how to interview over video—it certainly wasn't the norm like it is today. And in 2006, the technology was far more rudimentary, so much so that I had to find an office building that had the hardware I needed.

At the office, I found a dry erase board on wheels, and asked if I could wheel it into the conference room where I'd call in. The receptionist looked at me like I had six heads.

"What are you going to do with it?" she asked.

"I'm going to use it for my interview," I told her. She nodded her head and signaled for me to take it.

I set everything up, and my interviewer appeared on the screen. But she was uncomfortable from the start. She told me I didn't fit the exact spec Yankee had put out, and she wasn't sure where this would go. Sometimes in life, luck plays a role—that is, if you as an individual take advantage of the opportunity. I was prepared and ready.

Clearly, the search firm respected Drew enough to move forward with his recommendation, and I was grateful that he'd shared my name. It was proof that sometimes the biggest opportunities come from loose connections—members of your Personal Trust Community you might not even recognize as such.

"So, you tell me how this goes," she said. "Yankee Candle is a great and growing business. The wholesale business is looking for a dynamic leader to take it into the future. Tell me how you'll do it."

I uncapped my marker and began laying it all out on the white board, something I'd learned to do from the team at Russell. I explained what I'd do to understand the business in full, and then showed her—step by step—what we would need to do to enhance the financials and raise morale, and how I'd go about it with the team.

When I was done, she took a deep breath. "I have to tell you, I'm going to do something I've never done before. I'm going to submit your resume and profile because of what you just did. Don't get me wrong: I didn't fully understand all of it. But I'm intrigued enough that I want to see what happens."

I went through a series of interviews after that. The last one on the docket was with the company's COO, Harlan Kent. On the drive to meet everyone that day, I called Maggie. "Can you check to see what Yankee Candle's earnings were yesterday?" The first real "smartphone" wouldn't drop for another year, after all.

"Not good, Mike," she said. "They had less-than-stellar earnings." I figured it would be a tough day for an interview, but I didn't have a choice.

When I got to Harlan's office for the last interview, he asked how my day had gone. Then he dropped a big binder on his desk with a thunk. "Look, my son has a lacrosse game in an hour-and-a-half, and I work an hour and ten minutes from his school, so I don't have a lot of time. He walked me through the business and much of what was going on. "I just have one final question for you," he said.

Oh jeez, I thought, *this is not good.*

"What's one lesson you learned from your experience at Russell?"

I took a deep breath. "If senior leadership isn't aligned on the mission and direction of a business, it will struggle and fail to achieve success."

"Good answer," he said. "You see this book right here? We just went through a whole review with Wall Street. It was not an easy day. We have a business that needs to be reimagined. I hope whoever comes on can do that. Anyway, I gotta head out. It was good to meet you."

He shook my hand, and that was that.

Boy, maybe ten, fifteen minutes tops. That sucks, I thought. *It's probably not going to work out.*

A few days later, I called the search firm, and asked for the woman who had first interviewed me. I braced for the bad news. "You won't believe this: Harlan loved you!" she said.

"Honestly, I was there for less than fifteen minutes! He really only asked me one question."

"Well, it must have been enough. He enjoyed the conversation as did the leadership team. He wants you to come back. What did you think?"

"The guy left to go to his son's lacrosse game. I think that's pretty cool. I want to work for a guy like that—a guy who cares about his family," I said.

After all the initial interviews were done, I received a call from the woman at the search firm. "You're one of four finalists," she said. "Off the record? I'm freaking rooting for you! It is rare that someone who doesn't fit the original profile makes it through the first round, so I'm wishing you well."

Months passed. Despite my progress, Yankee Candle's process had been moving at a glacial pace. Spalding was still waiting for an answer as to whether I was interested in the role they'd described. And Maggie and I had made the decision to move back to Simsbury no matter what. It was the right decision for our girls. We even bought a house there, though I'd been unemployed for four months. (The real estate market in 2006—before the crash—was much looser, and you could buy a house without a job if lenders felt you were good for the money. I cannot imagine that happening today.)

I finally received a call from Yankee Candle requesting that I come up for a final meeting with the company's CEO, Craig Rydin, and the COO, Harlan Kent—the man who rushed out to get to his son's lacrosse game.

We met up at a restaurant in the Avon/Simsbury area of Connecticut. I enjoyed both of them very much, and from their description the position felt like a great fit for what I was looking for.

That said, I was stressed because the process had dragged on for several months. I knew I couldn't force this one, but I couldn't hold Spalding off any longer either. I was walking the fine line of pushing for a decision while also reminding myself that sometimes you have to "let the game come to you," as I'd learned in sports.

One of them asked me about the "other" job I was considering and where I stood with that. They obviously didn't want to make an offer only to find out I would reject it. Now that we had reached the final stage of the journey, I decided to share my thoughts. "Hold on a minute," I responded. "This process has dragged on for several months. This is the job I want. I'm the one waiting for a decision."

"Well, we heard you bought a house already. What were you thinking, buying a house without a job?"

I told them about the promise I'd made to our daughters before I took the role at Russell and reconfirmed after the job ended. It was Simsbury or bust.

"But the house is an hour and fifteen minutes from the office."

"My family matters more than the commute. This is the job I want."

Craig told me that he and Harlan lived in that area and did that commute themselves every day. It wasn't that bad, he said.

Then, he basically asked whether I would take the job if he offered it to me.

"Yes," I answered. That question made me feel like the job was mine, but you never know in these situations.

When the offer came through, my first order of business was to get up to speed on the company as a whole.

Yankee Candle had me learn the people and business before stepping into my role. I spent time with two people who to this day have been invaluable to me as colleagues, friends, and Personal Trust Community members: Martha LaCroix, the SVP of HR, and Dorrin Exford, the Director of Learning and Development. Both of them would invest in me and my development and help me grow the team and our capabilities. Two selfless people who I am grateful for to this day. The entire leadership team was supportive and invested time in helping me get ready for the role. It was a great group of people, and I was impressed by them right from the start.

I was also introduced to Predictive Index, a company that assesses individual and team behavior to help organizations align and optimize talent. I'd never been exposed to anything like that; no team I'd ever been a part of had cared about my unique characteristics and how to blend them with those of my team. Here, I was told I'd learn not only how I was wired, but also how I was motivated.

I was stunned by the accuracy of my results. Further, they were able to tell me where I'd thrive, where I'd be challenged with my team, and where I'd be pushed to grow.

Then, someone sat down with me and went through my roles and responsibilities, describing how my characteristics and work style—as determined by the Predictive Index—would affect my job, my interactions at work, and the senior leadership team at large. It was the first time I'd ever stopped to consider the individual and interpersonal experiences I'd had over the course of my career—why I got along so well with one person, felt frustrated by another's questions, why I'd made the decisions I made, and more.

I also got a chance to tour the Yankee Candle plant, get to know the leaders there, to find my footing before I stepped through the door of my office.

It was so different from the company initiations I'd had prior, where I was essentially handed a list of numbers to hit and told to make it happen.

The process was overwhelming in its own way. With so much information to sift through, I worried that the people working there were smarter than I was, that I wouldn't fit in, that I'd never catch on to the particular cadence and rhythm that were clearly already in place. There was also, of course, the issue of navigating completely unfamiliar territory.

Yankee Candle owned a company called Aroma Naturals and, one day, I got a calendar invite to attend their meeting. No one had mentioned it during my interviews—I didn't even know what Aroma Naturals was. When I arrived at the meeting, I learned something else I hadn't known. I was there to make decisions.

The team kicked off the meeting by explaining a series of new fragrances, describing the notes of each. The words seemed to swirl around the room, untethered and meaningless.

"How do you want to proceed?" Twenty-two heads turned in my direction.

I panicked. I had no idea. What was I supposed to say?

Thankfully, the presenter broke the silence. "Oh, you may be better off smelling the fragrances and deciding which ones you want to launch."

"Yeah, let's do that. That's a good idea," I said.

The presenter gestured for us to proceed to another room where there was a wall with little doors lined up along it—each about the height of a freezer, and half the width. The presenter demonstrated what to do, opening a little door and inhaling deeply.

I didn't know a bad fragrance from a good one. The only candles I'd burned to date had been on birthday cakes. Meanwhile, twenty-two people huddled around me as I opened the first door and imitated what I'd just seen. I felt the sweat drip down my back. I was directed to a second door, and opened it and sniffed, repeating the gestures I'd seen.

"Look, I don't know the product line very well. I'd be comfortable with either one of them," I said, attempting to keep my cool.

"Well, which top notes do you like best?" someone prodded, "How about the lemon-lime?"

"I prefer it, I think," I said, and they nodded solemnly.

After the meeting, I headed to Harlan's office. "I just sat in on an Aroma Naturals meeting. I don't know if I did it right or not—I don't know much about the brand," I said, explaining what had happened.

"What were you doing in that meeting?" he asked, confused but with a smile on his face.

"They wanted some direction on the brand…"

"My apologies. Let's have you stay out of those meetings. I'll handle it with the team going forward, and we can consider looping you in sometime down the road."

Harlan had my back, but I had to learn how to show up for him. Soon after, I got a valuable lesson in building trust, and it harkened back to my answer to Harlan's question during my first interview with him.

At some point during my first or second year, he was looking for the leadership team to put together some new ways to grow revenue and profit. When the preliminary work was done, he asked me to put together a plan and strategy to help improve the profitability of our iconic jar business in collaboration with the company's Senior VP of Operations, Paul Hill.

Since I was still learning the ropes, I followed Paul's lead. I didn't update Harlan very often, and just assumed that Paul would guide us. When it was time to present the strategy we had developed to the executive team, Paul felt it was best for me to share our ideas.

I got up in front of the group and began laying out what we had come up with. The team was asking question after question, rapid-fire. It felt as though the meeting was not going well. It certainly seemed as if I had failed to grasp the expectations. And as the sweat poured off me, I hit a nerve with Harlan— and not a good one. Mercifully, the meeting ended with the decision to consider the ideas at a later date.

Afterward, Harlan pulled me into his office. "What the hell are you doing?" he demanded.

"I'm so sorry," I said. "I know you asked Paul and me to come up with a strategy…"

"Mike, I'd prefer not to show up for a meeting and discuss ideas that you and I have not aligned on. Going forward, it would be helpful that we talk through your ideas ahead of time, especially when they're 'controversial.'"

I was visibly nervous. I worried that I'd be fired on the spot. I didn't trust myself yet—I didn't feel like I belonged.

"It's fine. it's fine," he said. "Just make sure I know where you're going so I can support you."

I could work with that. Going forward—more often than not—I made sure that if I had an idea, I would run it by him before sharing it with the group. That way, when we all came together as an executive team, he could be there for me.

With a solid system for communication, Harlan came to appreciate my willingness to tackle hard subjects and would periodically ask me to help him in those areas. When I had to address something tricky with the executive team, he would pull me aside and ask if I'd bring it up during our next meeting. That way, I could set it up, and he could drive it home.

I also got into the data very quickly. Our products were sold in more than 500 Yankee Candle retail stores, and distributed wholesale to 20,000 small gift stores, Bed Bath & Beyond, and other home stores. I realized that if I had intimate knowledge of what was happening on the retail side, I could share that information with our wholesale department, and vice versa. In our corporate office, the retail team occupied the first floor, the wholesale team was stationed on the second floor, and leadership was on the third floor. One day, I asked someone in wholesale if they'd ever asked retail if they were dealing with the same set of challenges we were facing.

"Well, they're on the first floor," they replied.

"I know that," I said, "I'm asking if you've ever gone down the stairs to ask them."

"Not really—no. We're on the second floor. They're on the first," they explained again, as if the limitations of such a structure were obvious. The conversation seemed to be futile, so I decided to walk down the stairs myself.

There, I found Steve Farley, who was the President of the retail division, and Hope Margala, who was Vice President and General Merchandise Manager. I explained that I was trying to get some answers about their side of the business. "I'm told we don't usually come down to ask questions," I finished.

They both practically fell off their chairs laughing. "Welcome to Yankee Candle," Steve said. We all became fast friends.

Hope knew the industry inside and out, and eventually came to work with me as VP of wholesale marketing. Because of our bond, she knew when I was struggling or when I needed help, and she was always there for me. Steve was one of the most enjoyable people I had ever met as a leader, and over time we grew to have a great relationship.

Also, as I mentioned, Martha LaCroix, the head of HR, became another member of my Personal Trust Community. She had been with Yankee a long time, and had become the keeper of the company's history. She willingly shared her knowledge and showed me tremendous compassion.

And of course, there was Dorrin Exford. Dorrin, Yankee's director of learning and development, helped me understand how to connect with my team. You'll remember that it began with the company Toastmasters group, where I finally let my guard down after so many years.

The first assignment was to share something personal that people didn't know. My adoption seemed like the right subject to cover. I was finally ready to tell my story. It had held me back for so long.

Maybe it's just time to say it and see what happens, I thought. I certainly had my fears, though. I worried that if people knew, they'd think less of me— that I'd feel even more vulnerable than I had in the past, and even more like I wanted to escape. But it also seemed like the perfect time and the perfect environment. It was a small group, 95 percent of whom I knew. And most of them were in HR. Their knack for understanding people made me feel safe. Dorrin agreed.

The rest, as you know from our first chapter, is history. But it's not where the story ends.

CENTRAL MA 015

JR SEP 2011 PM 3 L

JIMMY FUND WALK
SEPT 18 2011
WALK TO FIGHT CANCER

Mr. Michael Thorne
5 Shant Estate Dr.
West Simsbury, Ct. 06092

0609242101

Michael,
    I can't begin to describe the feelings in my heart being able to Send you (finally) a card for your birthday.
    Please know I am thinking of you as always and have a great day —
        Alice

...you will always be my son,
and I will always love you.

Happy Birthday
Enjoy the day
Alice

Alice's first birthday card to me

CHAPTER 8

"Takin' on a challenge is a lot like riding a horse. If you're comfortable while you're doin' it, you're probably doin' it wrong."
—Ted Lasso

They say a new broom sweeps clean. I had spent seven years at Yankee Candle. In 2013, the company was acquired by Jarden Corporation. Not long after, the CEO of Rawlings, Robert Parrish, reached out to our SVP of HR to inquire about the possibility of me joining his team (Rawlings was another one of Jarden's portfolio companies).

As much as I loved the job, location, and people at Yankee Candle, it was clear to me that things were going to change. Harlan had always been good at signaling, and in so many words, he'd told me that—no matter what Jarden said publicly—Yankee Candle was going to be a different company going forward. Although we discussed alternative roles within Yankee Candle, including exploring a newly created one with global scale, it was time. Time to move on. It was just a matter of choosing what made the most sense.

One day, I ran into Martha Lacroix—our SVP of HR—in the parking lot. She told me that Robert had been hounding her. "Please call him back," she said.

I had long loved Rawlings' brand, but I had reservations about going back to an industry I'd left seven years prior. I knew I had reached an important crossroads, and I wanted to be intentional about what I did next. *How do I apply what I learned during previous transformations?* I wondered.

Ultimately, I did speak to Robert. After our conversation, I went to visit the company and meet the executive team. Seeing the athletes plastered on the walls of the building, smelling the baseball gloves again, and meeting the team, I felt like the role and company would be a good fit.

Unfortunately, it meant I'd have to move to St. Louis. Having navigated multiple moves by that point, I knew it had to be on terms that worked for me and our family, or I would pursue something else.

Robert and I sat down and discussed what the agreement looked like, and I aligned with his vision for the role and the expectations pretty quickly. But there was one disconnect. More than my salary, I was concerned about the health of the company and the risk that Jarden would make changes that would make my role untenable.

No one else seemed to be worried, but I had seen this movie before and thought there was no way the current leadership team would be intact for very long. I wanted to make sure my family and I wouldn't end up in yet another difficult situation. I thought our conversation was confidential, but that wasn't the case.

Shortly after our discussion, I was working with Yankee Candle's sales team when a call came in, flashing Connecticut's 203 area code across my phone screen. Jim Lillie was the CEO of Jarden, and his assistant was on the other line. Jim wanted me to meet with him the next day.

Being that he was my new boss, I agreed to a morning meeting and rearranged my schedule to make it.

On the way home from work, I called Harlan. I told him what happened and asked if he had any idea what the meeting was about. "Just wear a sport coat and hear him out," he suggested.

Amidst all this internal upheaval, search firms were reaching out. They knew that changes were afoot, and they were looking to capitalize on them. As a result, I had other options to consider. A significant global role with a major retail/wholesale gift company, the beginnings of conversations with Under Armour, and other opportunities were bubbling in the background. It was unclear who was serious, and who was just kicking the tires, but a few recruiters were persistent—insisting that they needed answers soon.

Although it was highly stressful to think about making yet another change, it was also exciting to consider a fresh start. By then I was experienced enough to know that several opportunities tend to converge at once, thus "forcing" you to make a decision without perfect information.

As I prepared for my meeting with Jim, I decided that if Robert and I could agree on the compensation and benefits, Rawlings was the right role for me.

As always, Maggie and our kids were front and center of my mind. Maggie and I always made sure we were aligned on next steps and she had such good instincts and knew what to say at just the right time. I trusted her implicitly. We had decided that if Rawlings was it, we would work with that.

The next day, I arrived at Jarden Headquarters. I was led to a room filled with samples from all the brands Jarden owned, and I looked around as I waited for Jim. It was the first time I had ever had a real opportunity to process the power of the corporation. I was energized thinking about how cool it was to be a part of a diverse brand with global reach.

I was escorted into another room, where Jim met me. I could tell from the get-go that this wasn't going to be an easy conversation.

"I am not sure who you think you are," he started, "but I understand from Robert you have several demands of Rawlings for this role?"

Jim spent time telling me what an amazing company and brand Rawlings was, and how great the company was performing. "Do you know how many wealthy investors want to own this brand?" he said, attempting to emphasize what a privilege it would be to work for the company. He even brought one of Jarden's finance leaders in to "show" me how well Rawlings was performing. But I'd done my homework.

I respected what he was saying, but I'd also spent two days meeting with Rawlings' team, spoken to others in the industry, and knew I could rely on my instincts and discernment. What he was describing was in complete contrast to what I'd seen and heard. Either he was selling me, or he was naive to what was actually happening "on the ground."

I stood *my* ground and expressed my concerns about the financial and operational issues at Rawlings, and the risk of moving to St. Louis. I would say we "agreed to disagree," and he asked me if I would help evolve Rawlings' model, versus revolutionize it.

"Am I negotiating with you or Robert?" I asked.

In the end, we agreed to the majority of what I had negotiated already. It felt odd that he and I were deciding the terms of agreement, but he said he would talk to Robert, and I left there feeling like the move to St. Louis was a sure bet. It wasn't long after my discussion with Jim that Robert called. We talked through the terms of the agreement, namely that I would finish the fourth quarter at Yankee Candle and participate in a few Rawlings meetings along the way to prepare for the following year. Robert said he was totally exasperated with the "arrangement," yet deep down I sensed he was thrilled to have me on the team.

Sure enough, when I attended Robert's fourth-quarter meeting, I learned that Rawlings' short-term future was going to be very rocky, and that Yankee Candle would become a fundamentally different company.

The new year rolled around, and I found myself sitting in a major meeting with Jarden's leadership team at Rawlings' headquarters. I remember it as if it were yesterday. We were not prepared for the challenges coming our way.

What was meant to be a multi-day review of the business turned into a ninety-minute beat down unlike I'd ever been a part of.

I remember sitting at the end of a large table in the Rawlings showroom and watching the meeting unfold. Robert began talking about the company's contract with the NFL, but things went downhill almost immediately. Before I knew it, we were given a warning to get our shit together and told there would be a follow-up scheduled to review expectations.

Right then, Ian, Jarden's CFO, turned to me. "Mike, since you're the new guy here, what do you think?"

Fortunately, I had prepared an answer ahead of time. "Ian, there are a lot of great people here. We've got a great brand and we just need some process discipline," I said.

"That is the smartest thing I've heard since we started," he said. And with that, we were dismissed.

As I drove home that night, I realized I was seeing the same patterns at Rawlings that had unfolded at Spalding and Russell and, to a much lesser extent, Yankee Candle. Spalding had challenging financials, along with morale issues. Yankee Candle had a terrific culture and a caring leadership team, but had some morale issues in the wholesale division when I arrived. The one common denominator was people.

Most companies focus much of their energy on financial P&L (profit and loss), while the big multiplier of growth is cultural P&L (people and listening). When you can do both well, the company thrives. To truly transform companies, you need to first listen to the stories of the employees, and when you do, they will move from compliance and survival mode to commitment and thriving mode.

During my first three to six months at Rawlings, we spent a lot of time on both financial and cultural P&L. At the end of our first sales meeting, and a few drinks in, Mike Thompson, a long-time, legendary executive at Rawlings, grabbed me around the neck and said, "Thorney, you've brought our mojo back." To me, it was proof that we were headed in the right direction, but I was sure we were far from out of the woods.

That first year, we continued to struggle and Jarden lost patience. The company ultimately changed CEOs, bringing in Mike Zlacket—a former senior executive for our competitor, Easton Baseball. That change was predictable, given the meetings we had and the pressure on Robert. Further, knowing that Mike had a senior head of sales—Bobby—who was also one of his best friends, I was sure my time at Rawlings would end at some point. Having been in roles where change is afoot, as a leader it is logical to get a few people who know you and understand you in seats that are critical to your success, and Mike would certainly consider getting "his guy" in when it came to sales. That said, the team was doing a good job transforming the brand and I was confident we were heading in the right direction.

There were a number of other signs, but everything came to a head after one of our first quarterly reviews with Mike Zlacket as CEO. Mike had requested that I meet with him, and after I arrived, he asked, "How long have you been with the company?"

"About a year," I responded.

"You know a lot about the company. I'm impressed."

"Thank you," I said.

He told me that while he appreciated how much time I spent looking to develop people, I also could get caught up in complaints, looking for areas to change, and general drama. "We don't have time for all that," he said. As I left the office and marinated over the conversation, I realized he was right. I felt there was a lot to fix, but there was a time and place to address the issues at hand, and I had to recalibrate my approach. We needed to get better, but by constantly pushing for change, I risked demoralizing people and undermining what I was trying to do.

Mike also had other ways to assess who was a good fit for his team, and I could see that there was a discrepancy between how we approached things. Mike would often take us on "bonding" experiences to give him a sense of the team dynamics—a trip to a winery, riding horses, and other activities Mike enjoyed. I'm not sure I was a good cultural fit.

Within a year, I found myself facing another request to meet Mike in his office, this time with our SVP of HR.

Just before the meeting, I called Maggie. "I'm pretty sure this is it," I told her. I sat in my office for several minutes and reflected on the time I'd spent there, what I learned from it all, and what might be next. Then, I proceeded to Mike's office.

He couldn't have been more professional as he delivered the inevitable, and I fully respected his decision.

Then, serendipitously, I got a call from a search firm. The firm had been hired by a private equity company to find the next leader of a multifaceted sports apparel company. I was curious but also concerned about getting involved with another business owned by a private equity firm. In my experience, when private equity came into a business, everything changed. The numbers became king, trumping everything else—including culture. I didn't want to find myself in the same situation I was trying to leave. But it sounded compelling.

The company founder had sold the business to two bankers who had done a remarkable job rebuilding the business and company, including its financials, to date. They had turned around and sold the business to the private equity firm, and at some point, intended to leave themselves. I'd have the chance to be involved in helping run a company again—and one in the manufacturing space at that, an area of the industry I loved.

The company had an interesting strategy too: their goal was to be *the* high-end performance apparel supplier for non-revenue producing sports, Olympic heavyweights like wrestling, swimming, and gymnastics. It had taken up residence in a Northeast blue-collar town, revitalizing it with new opportunities for the locals. All of that intrigued me.

In looking over my Personal Trust Community, there was someone I felt could provide some much-needed perspective: Eddie Bender, who had been a senior executive at Spalding when I was there. He was on the outskirts of my trust community, someone I didn't interact with often but whose perspective and opinion I valued. He processed the opportunity with me, giving me feedback on what he knew about the firm that owned the business, the company, and the role itself.

Over the years, I learned to really do my homework, digging into the backgrounds of my potential colleagues. I look for clues about what they value and how they'll act when the going gets tough. But this time, I didn't. Caught up in the potential to take the reins of a business, I forged ahead.

But I rushed into it, without exploring my true passions and what I had learned from my prior experiences. We had been building a beautiful home in Saco, Maine, on the ocean, and felt that we were putting down roots with that decision. It was time to be patient and wait for the right opportunity to come along, but I wasn't.

I had just lost my job at Rawlings, and I felt like I needed to dive back into another business. I'd been speaking with another sports brand in another state, but ultimately chose to pull the trigger there.

It was the middle of winter when I had my last interview—a session with a guy named Mike who worked for the private equity firm. I was at my kitchen table in Maine, and it felt like it was about twenty degrees below zero. I liked Mike right away, and he seemed very knowledgeable. I was excited by the way he talked about the opportunity, and though it was freezing both inside the house and out, our conversation made me feel warm. I was sold. So, I signed on without meeting more of the staff or walking the floor. Without asking more people more questions.

The company would put my wife and I up in a fully furnished apartment near the office, and we could look for a permanent place once I settled in at work. Meanwhile, we'd keep the house in Maine.

Soon after I started the job, I began to see how much I'd missed by joining without asking more questions. Mike had a unique approach to leadership: pitting two leaders against each other to see who'd rise to the top. In meetings, he'd challenge us, egging us on until someone took the bait. He would call us two "Ferraris," and as I learned later, he felt this was the best way to see who would win the race.

I noticed, too, that the leadership team seemed to be stacked with "friends" of the two bankers—people who likely wouldn't question decisions. There was nothing wrong with that, just something that, from my experience, would not lead to the kinds of decisions and behaviors I looked for in a company.

The business had done remarkably well, and the bankers at the helm—along with the leadership team—had done an excellent job building the future. They were both supportive of me acclimating to the business. Unfortunately, the early red flags made me skeptical about whether I was a good fit for the organization. The question at hand wasn't about capabilities; it was more about values and style.

Then, the signs became undeniable. Within the first few months of my arrival, a woman in the marketing and product department knocked on my door. "Come in," I said, looking up from my computer screen.

She closed the door behind her and sat down. "I assume you're here to improve the culture and overall 'people' issues here?" she said.

"What do you mean? What's going on?" I asked.

She began to provide some insights into the history of the company and what had gone on over the last few years, which helped me gain perspective on the situation and the challenges ahead. Not only was I struggling to find my footing on the business side of things; I was beginning to realize that I had missed important cues when it came to the culture.

I thanked her for coming to me, and when she left, I put my head in my hands. I knew I needed to dig deeper into these issues, to find someone else who might be able to give me some additional insight—someone who wasn't part of the upper echelons of the organization.

I tried to talk to the folks at the firm that hired me, but those conversations didn't go very far.

One piece of advice was, "Just take control. That's what we hired you to do." But it didn't seem that easy.

Eventually, I decided to go to lunch with a respected leader within the organization. After we sat down, I explained what I'd been hearing and feeling.

He played dumb to it all, acting as if I were on another planet. But it was clear that something was happening behind the scenes, and that it didn't sit well with me or fit with my style. I had deep respect for the company's leaders and what they'd built—a growth business model with a moat that would allow it to thrive for the long haul. It was very compelling, and I didn't want to feel like I was just trying to fit in, but another lesson I'd learned was weighing on my mind. You need to feel as though you belong to bring your full self to the table, in business and beyond.

Now I was pretty sure it wasn't going to work. But I was scared to move on so quickly. *What if things worked out and I could lead the company some day? What would I do next? What would my friends and family think?*

Regardless, I had to say something about how I was feeling. I met with one of the CEOs and let him know what was on my mind. I wasn't sure I belonged there or that I could effectively participate in the company culture. He attempted to take me through his vision using a dry-erase board, but things still weren't adding up for me.

Soon after, I took a work trip to California where I had been working with Bo Eason and his team. I scheduled lunch with one of my Personal Trust Community members, Tim Dixon, who was there for work too. I told him about everything I was grappling with. "I don't know what to do," I finished.

"Are you doing what you want to do?" he asked, "or are you doing what you need to do?"

"What do you mean?"

"Well, sometimes what you want to do and what you need to do are very different. You might be hanging onto this job because you *want* to tell your friends that you'll ultimately have the opportunity to be the CEO of this company. Your value is based on titles and income versus what you care about. But you are someone who thrives in environments and cultures where people matter and you feel valued. You enjoy rallying people and inspiring them to take action. It seems like you're just tolerating all this, and you're unhappy as a result. It sounds like you don't belong there, but you're holding on because you feel like if you don't, everyone's going to wonder, 'What happened to Mike?' But only you can determine whether that's the case."

"What would it mean to do what I need to do?" I asked him.

"Well, what are your values? What's important to you? What do you care about? If all that matters to you is a big title and a paycheck to go with it, then you're doing what you need to do. But if you decide that the way they're operating doesn't align with your values—with what you need out of a job or a company—you've got to tell them it's just not a good fit. You've got to walk away."

I flew home that night on a redeye. When I got back early Monday morning, Maggie echoed Tim's advice. "Do what you think is right," she said.

It wasn't an easy decision. About a week prior, we had purchased a condo near my new job and paid cash for it—even though, deep down, I knew we shouldn't have. It was a cool place, near the action downtown. We thought we would enjoy being able to walk to activities. But noise from the neighborhood—a bar, a pizza parlor, a gym—filtered in at all hours. Even my kids had questioned the decision, saying that the place just didn't feel like us. But I was making these choices because I didn't want to give up. Up until that point, I worried about how leaving would reflect on me above all else. That had to change.

That night, I emailed the CEOs. *I'd love to meet with you tomorrow*, I wrote.

How about nine o' clock? they responded.

That morning, I met them in the conference room and placed my keys on the table.

"What's going on?" one of them asked.

"Look, I take 100 percent of the blame here. I didn't do a good job vetting the position before I signed on. You've got a very profitable business, and the private equity firm has a clear sense of what they want to do next. I just don't feel like it's a good fit for me personally. And the longer I'm here, the harder it will be for you to make it work long term, and the less productive I'll be. I'm sorry to end things this way."

They both seemed surprised. "This isn't going to be good for you," one said. "You just moved here. What are you gonna do with the condo?"

"Honestly? I don't have a good answer for that right now. I just know this isn't a good fit for me, and that I won't be a good fit for you either based on where you're going."

"We're sorry to hear that," they said. There wasn't really anything else to say.

Right afterward, I called Mike from the private equity company to tell him what I'd decided. He was upset that I was bailing after just a handful of months, but I explained how I'd come to my decision, and everything I'd seen and heard along the way. He had a wealth of experience and I had learned a lot from him in a short time. That said, I shared some of my concerns around the culture.

He told me he didn't agree with what I'd said, but that he'd look into it.

"I'm going to put it in writing," I said. "If you choose to sue me because I put it in writing, I just ask that you let me know ahead of time. That's all I ask. But I'll defend what I believe until the very end."

After I left the office, I drove back to the condo. We hadn't really moved in yet. Everything was still dusty, and we'd brought in just a few pieces of furniture—a bed, a lone rocking chair, in the living room, a TV we'd perched on the mantle. I sat in that rocking chair for a while, listening to its creak and the sounds from the street echo off the empty walls. *What am I going to do next?* I wondered. I couldn't believe I was in this situation yet again. *Look, things happen for a reason,* I told myself.

Soon after, I emailed my former boss at Yankee, Harlan Kent, just to let him know what happened. He had moved on by then and encountered his own challenges along the way. Lo and behold, he called me the next day, as I was making the drive from Pennsylvania to Maine, my car stuffed with an assortment of boxes. "I got your message. Why don't we get together next week?"

"What's going on?"

He had just taken over as CEO of Performance Sports Group, which included Bauer Hockey, two small lacrosse brands, and Easton Baseball, and was based in New Hampshire—about forty-five minutes from my house in Maine.

He had always been a leader I trusted, and I knew we shared very similar values when it came to business and culture, so I was interested in seeing what he had to say.

On the long drive to his office the following week, I realized that jumping into another business in need of reimagining and change probably wasn't a good idea. I needed time to consider what Tim said: doing what I wanted to do versus what I needed to do. With that in mind, I showed up at Harlan's office.

After hearing what Harlan was looking for, I realized I wanted to help, but in my own way. I don't want to come on full time," I told him. "I just can't do it. I don't want to end up in the situation I just got out of. I appreciate you, and I'm happy to help. But it has to be some sort of consulting role." I didn't know anything about consulting, but I knew I could be helpful. Everything else, I was sure I could figure out. Harlan nodded.

"If you bring me on, though, I'm going to do it my way. It's not going to be all that Dartmouth-Harvard-MBA stuff—no fancy finance, no charts and graphs," I said with a laugh. "So if that's what you're looking for, don't hire me to do this. I'm going to walk around with a pen and a notepad. I'll talk to the people in the trenches—in supply chain, sales, brand, planning, distribution, in customer service—and ask for their stories and the answers to a few simple questions."

"Do it the way you want to do it. I just need you here."

Before I left, Harlan hugged me. "I'm so excited," he said, "I look forward to having you here helping us rebuild the business." He'd never hugged me in the seven years I'd worked for him, and maybe that should have been an indicator of how challenging things would be!

My next order of business was for us to sell the condo we had just bought. I called our real estate agent, who thought we were out of our minds, but that ended up working out too. We were able to sell it for just a little more than we'd paid.

Not too long after all this, I was back in Maine and grabbed the mail—as I always do. In the stack was a letter from my former employer. The company was looking to help me through the transition, a gesture I very much appreciated. It was, in essence, a way to help offset the costs of the transition along with a non-disclosure agreement. Pretty standard stuff, but a nice gesture nonetheless.

There was paperwork to fill out and sign. I took the packet they'd sent over to the couch and began going through it. Maggie was there too, and our middle daughter, Sarah, was in the kitchen. I could see her from where I sat.

Among the documents was a non-disclosure agreement. I showed my wife the form. "How do I sign this in good conscience? What does it convey to our kids?" I asked, gesturing toward Sarah.

Neither of us could come up with a good answer. So, I never signed the papers. I didn't submit them and passed on any financial support during the transition. I told my kids I'd opted out too. Some time later, they'd tell me that my decision solidified for them that values matter most—that they were proud of me for the choice I made.

A few years later, the media would shine a light on the corruption and abuse that had been running rampant through the gymnastics industry, affecting virtually everyone involved—including Olympic athletes—for decades. We would watch and read in horror about what these athletes had experienced at the hands of people they were supposed to be able to trust. It was stunning in scope, but even more so in that people at the highest level chose "winning" over people.

I was disappointed in the choices I had made, the things I'd overlooked in deciding to take the job. I was frustrated that I couldn't fix it too. Those three months are absent from my resume, a blip in time. But in the end, I learned a lot about myself and decision-making, and that made the whole ordeal feel worth the trouble. Many times, to transform, we must go through discomfort.

Finally, I began to drown out the voices that weren't helpful—even some who were close to me, people who questioned me for changing jobs or making particular choices that felt right to me—and tapping into the people who could provide valuable insight during turbulent times. I became even more deliberate about who I let into my Personal Trust Community, and when I reached out to them. I realized that there were people I could call tomorrow for a beer or a cup of coffee—people I could talk to about life and kids in a general fashion. But they weren't necessarily the same people I could or should reach out to when an emotional, intellectual, or spiritual issue arose; they just weren't equipped to support me in those areas. Further, I realized how their responses made me feel: like that nine-year-old boy, unsure that I belonged anywhere at all. Just as I had done in college, I got good at drawing a line.

I also made sure that, when I chose to let someone in, I *really* let them in. I worked to quiet the fears that I had to depend on others because I wasn't good enough and instead recognized the value in their unique perspectives. I got vulnerable.

And I made sure I was asking *myself* the right questions any time I was considering a transition, big or small.

Even today, I keep Tim's queries at the forefront of my decision-making process. Whenever I'm considering an opportunity, I begin by asking myself, "What do I want to do? What do I need to do?"

Maggie and I spending time taking a walk together

Celtics/Warriors 2019 game with my best friend

CHAPTER 9

"You gotta let go of all of the past, you know, bring the good parts forward, forget about the negative stuff, and go on. Because whenever you get hung up and locked into the past, you're robbing yourself of the present....and definitely the future for sure."
—Quincy Jones

I was ready for the next phase of my career. I planned to take all the skills, tools, and resources I had acquired over the course of my professional life and use them to support those who had the drive and desire to make an impact, but lacked the know-how—like nonprofits and small and mid-size businesses.

My first step, I figured, was to build a website. I found a company to help me put it all together, one that a previous colleague had used for a similar transition. They were located out west, and that meant most of our meetings took place virtually or by phone.

I worked through all the paperwork they sent me—a questionnaire with what felt like a million inquiries, and exercise after exercise. But nothing the designers proposed felt right. Months went by, and we still hadn't crossed the finish line.

It occurred to me that, if I needed someone to truly "get" me, I might need to look in my own backyard. After my last work transition, Maggie and

I had decided to plant our flag in Maine. If I was going to build a business here, and truly settle in one place, maybe I needed a local developer to help me out.

Soon after, I found a Maine-based developer who seemed to understand what I was after—Judy Wood of Wood and Company. When I spoke to her, she was probing and direct and I liked her style. We ended up meeting in her office after our initial call, and she seemed to assess my needs without judgment. She also projected a cool confidence that she would get this done.

"What's the name of the company, Mike?" she asked.

That was my biggest issue: I had no idea at the time. I decided that I'd let the name come to me and work with her on the other aspects of the brand first. Then, without the anxiety of trying to find the right fit, it all came to me at once.

At 3:45am, I bolted awake. Two words kept running through my mind: *Ask Inside, Ask Inside, Ask Inside.* That was it, the name of my operation! It made so much sense, given my belief about how individuals, leaders, and businesses should think about how to be their best. When one is unsure of what to do, they should *ask inside*, digging deep to identify the best way to proceed. When people align their mind and heart, they make better decisions. Maggie was sleeping soundly beside me, and it took a lot of restraint not to wake her up to tell her what I'd just come up with. She likely would have been less enthused than I was!

Judy built my logo and website, and I was ready to go.

With the sale of the condo behind me, and my new business name squared away, I could focus on helping Harlan with the business challenges he was facing. He had been a great boss, mentor, and friend to me, and so our work together felt particularly purposeful. I owed Harlan all I had in me.

Harlan was running Performance Sports Group, a global public company made up of several iconic sports brands like Bauer Hockey and Easton Baseball along with two smaller, yet successful Lacrosse brands. As a public company, it intended to grow by buying innovative brands and leveraging the various expertise of the leaders across each one. In June of 2014, Performance Sports Group launched its IPO at $15.50 a share, raising $125 million. After peaking at $20 on May 11, 2015, the stock crashed on poor sales, hitting less than $3 a share.

The businesses were struggling, and the stock was under so much pressure that many were worried about its future. The powers that be decided to change Performance Sports Group's leadership. That's when Harlan was brought in and tasked with rebuilding it. He soon found that the situation was more difficult than he had anticipated. In fact, by the time I arrived in late spring of 2016, it was dire. Layoffs appeared very likely.

For the first time in my life, I'd have the chance to test out my consulting ideas on a business. I was excited. The business itself aligned with my interests, and Harlan was supportive. My strategy felt so simple, yet powerful. I'd walk around with my notebook asking people three questions:

What do we do well and should do more of?
What should we do less of or not at all?
How can I help you personally and professionally?

I figured the strategy would help me quickly gain a sense of where the organization was and identify any themes. Armed with that information, I could make improvements that would rebuild morale back and ultimately help people see that there was a light at the end of the tunnel.

So, that's what I did. And soon after, people began to share their stories. Trust was building.

I also saw something play out that I'd observed in numerous other businesses over the years. In due time, you learn who the "culture carriers" are in an organization, the people who everyone trusts—which is rarely dictated by title. Those are the people who can help leaders implement necessary transitions.

Over the course of my career, I'd learned that people want more than just a job and a paycheck. They want to know you care about them. Walking around with my notebook and pen, I learned about the struggles the team was facing—big and small.

One issue seemed like it would be particularly easy to fix. Every time a customer called the corporate desk, the computers shut down. That meant whoever was staffing it couldn't solve the problem at hand. It was extremely frustrating, and it had been happening for months.

"Have you told anyone about this?" I asked one of the culture carriers.

"We've mentioned it, but no one seemed to care," I was told.

I went to see Paul, the Senior VP of IT. When I explained what was happening, he was shocked. "That can't be true," he said. "No one's ever said anything to me."

"The team told me no one would listen," I replied.

Each time I asked people to tell me their story, walls seemed to break down and communication began to flow. Moreover, I saw what I'd always believed played out in real time: everyone just wanted to be valued. When they felt they were appreciated, their performance improved tenfold.

My initial time there was spent working on the Bauer brand and the "front end of the business," and it felt like we were getting through some of the internal roadblocks. But things were quickly unraveling behind the scenes. All of this is a public record, so I won't waste print here. You can read it for yourself. Suffice to say, there were a lot of misguided decisions made, inherited by Harlan and his team, and in my experience when arrogance and ignorance take over a company, it's almost guaranteed to fall apart. Harlan had walked into a very difficult situation that seemed to become more challenging every day.

One day, I was introduced to Todd Harman, the Executive Vice President and General Manager of Easton, and asked to spend time with him, since I had some experience with Rawlings and the space overall. Todd was a great guy and I enjoyed the conversation immensely, but I left troubled. The Easton brand always seemed to me to be a great family-owned business, but when Performance Sports Group purchased it, the culture changed—as did the atmosphere. Performance Sports Group appeared to drive direction and strategy from New Hampshire, when Easton was sitting in the Mecca of baseball in California. That didn't make sense. Todd was frustrated, and I could understand why. At the time, though, there was more than enough to do with Bauer, so I offered Todd my help if he needed it down the road and went on my way.

But the situation at Easton Baseball, combined with the unraveling of Performance Sports Group's entire portfolio, led to the decision to take the company bankrupt. It was a stunning fall, for sure.

Harlan called me into his office and asked me to take on the challenge of bringing the Easton brand through the bankruptcy process while he worked on the overall business. But there was another layer of complication: he wanted me to do it in California.

Now, I tried to process how coming in to help him in New Hampshire as a consultant—just forty-five minutes from my home—had turned into a potential move to California. Anyone who knows Harlan knows that he doesn't ask you to let him know what you think; rather, he presents a decision he's already made. It's a tendency I'd always admired, because it shows the trust and faith he had in others' leadership abilities.

"I live on the ocean here on the east coast, not the west coast," I told him in jest.

"Talk to Maggie," he said. "I need you to do this. It won't be forever." Famous last words....

Despite this particular complication, I was excited by the opportunity. I'd run divisions of major companies before, but never a whole company—nor one going through a bankruptcy. One of the key calculations for me was whether going to California aligned with my new ethos of doing what I wanted to do, versus doing what I needed to do. Was I taking this on to prove my self-worth again?

When I started Ask Inside, I intended to begin a new, more purposeful journey—one focused on helping others rather than building my career. It had become clear to me that aligning my mind and my heart enabled me to make better decisions. Before then, I would have been preoccupied with what everyone else would think of me and how my choices would be perceived. The thought of deciding what made sense via a heart-centered instead of a fear-based one was extraordinary.

The second part of the equation was the people. I had done some homework on the business and the people and realized that, though they had already been through a lot, Easton was still a powerhouse when it came to baseball bat sales. Clearly it had some strong people working on the business. Having spent time with the Bauer organization, and knowing enough about Easton, I also felt the Easton team was made up of my kind of people. They cared deeply about the brands, wanted to succeed, and just needed some clarity when it came to purpose and direction.

So, I agreed to help.

What I didn't foresee was the complexity of a bankruptcy, the magnitude of navigating all the moving parts and constraints, and the impact of all that on how people would respond.

The day I came in—Halloween, of all days—we announced the bankruptcy. Harlan delivered the news and then introduced me to everyone at Easton over the phone. He explained further that he didn't know how long I'd be there. "Mike will have the reins for as long as it takes," he told the group. I wondered how they'd take to a new leader from Maine.

Due to bankruptcy laws and other issues, I couldn't have a president or CEO title, which didn't seem like a big deal at the time. But in a few months, I would learn that the title mattered to others. People wanted to know whether I was a puppet, or whether I really had the decision-making power. That surprised me, but it also spoke to how people who have been through a lot of change craved stability. Having a new leader from Maine who came on without a president's title, all while the company was going through a bankruptcy didn't exactly instill confidence. Eventually, I talked to Harlan and asked if I could just explain the decision not to name me president. I knew being honest and transparent with the team would build trust going forward. The team wasn't exactly happy to meet me, and reasonably so. But I was ready to address their issues while managing the challenges of bankruptcy and the sale of the business.

Soon after I arrived, I employed my consulting strategy, asking to meet with as many people as possible, going deep and making space for people to share their stories. At the same time, I was challenged to find cost savings for the business and rebuild revenue. It felt a lot like driving a car ninety miles down the highway, taking a left turn and changing the tire all at once. Despite that, it was an amazing experience and rewarding to see people work through all the challenges together, to show up every day determined to get back to a lower-stakes work environment.

I very quickly observed that the team yearned to go back to the way things were before PSG bought them and that they sensed or hoped I would only be there a short time. It didn't take a genius to realize they were just tolerating me as the leader, and that they would comply with the expectations but wouldn't commit. After all, who knew how long I'd be there? Meanwhile,

I couldn't commit to them either, because there was no certainty on my end. It was an interesting dance, to say the least.

What I learned, though, was that being authentic and keeping everyone's best interest in mind would ultimately win the day. I couldn't be someone I wasn't and throughout my time there, people questioned my approaches, challenged my thinking, and hoped that someone else would lead them back to the old glory days. To make it through, I kept returning to my purpose (*Am I doing what I want or need to do?*) and am I leading with my mind and my heart, or not? When I reflected on it, I realized I was. That allowed me to stay confident. Over time, I sensed that people were coming around. They began to feel that I wasn't just there to be a mercenary for the "New Hampshire people," that I was there to help and build a better future for them.

While I couldn't commit entirely, I decided to find a slightly more permanent living situation. I had started out in hotels, but I'd gotten tired of packing up and moving from one to another. So, in December, I found an apartment near Easton's offices in Thousand Oaks. I think the actual town was Aurora Hills. Between working through a fresh set of bat regulations implemented by the industry, building a new financial model, learning the business, building morale, and hosting potential buyers for the business, it was a very busy time.

All the while, I was commuting back to Maine every twelve or thirteen days, where I'd log a weekend with Maggie and turn around. Occasionally, I would head to Bauer's corporate office in New Hampshire and provide an update. All in all, it was a lonely existence. I didn't establish myself in California, because I didn't know how long I would be there. And I spent so much of my downtime in transit. Everyone I worked with had their own well-established lives, but I was just a short-termer. It was exhausting, but my sense of purpose kept me going.

After we negotiated the details of the sale at the end of February, I got an interesting call from one of the new owners. He wanted to visit me in California. I had met him once before in New Hampshire and he was constantly probing me with questions as to why someone who lived in Maine would be working on a business in California. I figured early on that he wasn't a fan of me and assumed I was lobbying to run Easton from New Hampshire.

Though it had been early on in the exploration phase, I'd left my one-on-one with him feeling that things probably wouldn't end well.

Months later, after pouring all I had into building a better future for Easton, I had grown interested in staying on full-time. It seemed crazy at first, but after devoting so much time to rebuilding morale, establishing a viable financial plan, and getting the company on stable ground, it was hard to walk away.

When he came to visit we were about to close things out, and the idea of sticking around had been occupying more and more of my brain space. "To be honest, Mike," he said, "I don't think you're fit to run this operation. I just met with the group yesterday, and team morale hasn't improved much."

I kept my composure, but I couldn't help but laugh to myself. How absurd and arrogant to think that after just four months of being on site—which followed more than two years of mismanagement, bankruptcy, and layoffs and the threat of even more—anyone could have had a significant impact on morale. He went on to critique a few more things about the way I'd led, including what he presumed to be my desire to move the business to New Hampshire. When he finished, I said in so many words, "With all due respect, I completely disagree with the idea of moving the company to New Hampshire. This is the mecca of baseball." Then, I delivered a vision for the brand going forward. It included keeping the people employed, the head-quarters where they were, and—most importantly—the business run from California and not New Hampshire. The cultures were just too different. He looked at me and said, "I will let you know" and off he went.

The moment he left I was disappointed, but not surprised, that someone could draw conclusions about my ability as a leader with one sweep of the office. He hadn't seen any of the nuance in what I'd done. I was also comfortable enough in my own skin to know that there was very little I could do to change his opinion. And as much as I would have enjoyed running that business, it was clear from that meeting there was another plan already under way. I also knew from my conversations with the team that there were a few very influential people at Easton that wanted Tony Palma, the former CEO and friend of the Easton Family, to lead things going forward.

Sure enough, I got a response a few days later. It read, "We are aligned." Aligned on what, I wasn't quite sure. Around the same time, it became obvious Harlan wouldn't be staying on long-term either, so I decided to let the chips fall where they may. It was a great experience and I looked forward to what "next" would look like.

Eventually, I was asked to stay on until the new owners could find a permanent CEO. By then, everyone knew that they were negotiating with Tony Palma, and they finally landed on a start date: June 2017. Meanwhile, Mathew Veedon, our CFO; Dave Lockridge, our VP of Sales; and several others were helping me shape the business strategy going forward. I am forever grateful for them and others who put in the time necessary to help to solidify Easton's future—all without being sure when it would end.

On Tony's first day, I met with him and I believe we went to lunch also. He listened to my perspective on the business, the recommendations the team and I had put together, and a few additional insights that I offered. There would be a meeting to announce Tony as the new CEO soon after.

Before what I thought was our last meeting to review the state of the business, I packed everything up and prepared to go back home to Maine. As I zipped up my backpack, Tony came by to ask me to come to the meeting when they would announce his return. I was hesitant; I thought it would be awkward. I'd put in my time, and now I could just fade out. But he insisted.

When leadership announced that he would be coming back, the whole room erupted into cheers. Tony said how pleased he was to be back, and then thanked me for all that I had done. I got the golf clap—a polite smattering of applause that dissipated after a few seconds.

And then the new owners spoke: "We want to make it clear that if it weren't for Mike, many of you would not have a job. Mike insisted that we keep things in California, since it's the baseball mecca of the country." After that, I got a much louder reception. And they were right—there had been a lot of people who were against the decisions we had made since the beginning. It was a small gesture, yet it was clear that investing time in both sides of a business (P&L business and P&L people/listening) matters.

After the meeting, I grabbed my backpack from my office and began to walk toward the door. It had been more than eight months, and I was ready to be in Maine for good.

"Hold up, Mike," I heard. There were several members of the leadership team standing there. One of them said, "You know, the first couple of months you were here, we had no idea what the hell you were doing—or even if you cared about us. But we've learned more from you in the time you've been out here than we learned in the last five years. Thank you for everything, including standing up for us." I shook everyone's hand, and even exchanged a few hugs before heading out into the sunshine.

It had been a great experience and another learning opportunity. Taking a company through a bankruptcy, selling it, and keeping the team intact was an accomplishment, but it wasn't quite as fulfilling as I hoped it would be. At the end of all those months, I felt empty. I had no idea whether all the work I'd put in to devise a strategy would be implemented. I wasn't sure consulting would feel as purposeful as I'd wanted.

But after I left, the cards began to arrive—notes from people on the team, even those who didn't seem to like me very much. One of the cards was from an engineer who hadn't been a big fan of mine while I was there. "Mike," he wrote, "you were the one person who stood toe-to-toe with the other guys on behalf of Easton. Thank you."

I knew I was onto something. From then on, before I took a consulting role, I shared my spiel with the team. "I'm an acquired taste. See this notebook here? I'm going to go around the building, ask people for their stories, pose some questions, and write down their answers. If you're going to hire me, you need to be okay with that." I led with that explanation, rather than my expertise.

"How long will that take?" they often asked.

"As long as it takes," I'd reply.

When the leaders of legacy businesses brought me on, I'd reimagine where they could go, and what they could do to support their people first and foremost.

One day, my phone rang, and Joe Fields was on the line. I'd worked with Joe in Tennessee, and I'd always admired and respected him. He told me he had taken over a synthetic turf company in Georgia called TenCate Grass not too long before then and was looking for some help entering into the northeast market. They had a distributor in Saco, Maine, and wanted to know if I might be interested in helping with them.

Again, I applied my filter (*What do I want to do versus what do I need to do?*) and saw this as another opportunity to give back to someone who had always been a good mentor and sounding board for me over the years. It felt like another opportunity to pay someone back who had taught me so much earlier in my career. After some back and forth, I decided to travel to the company's sales meeting in Kansas City to meet the team and explore whether a position there might make sense. Eventually, I agreed to a consulting role. I enjoyed working with Joe again. He is a force of nature and operates with supreme confidence and command. It felt almost as if I was on a string he'd pull at will. I'd move with him, even if I didn't fully understand the direction. I knew by then that there was always a method to his approach. I knew that Joe always tried to stay one step ahead of the game and, like a good Army guy that he had always been, if he sensed danger he would stamp it out. It was part of the fun and challenge of working with him.

Over time, my role evolved, and I became an employee. We built a business in the northeast, helped put together a plan and strategy for the field businesses that had been purchased and things seemed to be going well. And one day, I had a choice to make: I could join the company in a full-time capacity in a new role, or move on. Joe needed someone to take on the Challenger Turf brand. After multiple conversations with Joe and my wife, I found myself sitting in our small sunroom here in Maine looking out at the ocean and thinking *How great would it be to take all I've learned, apply it directly to a company, and run it as CEO?* Being able to put my mind-heart leadership mindset into practice for real was exciting despite all the risks in front of me. The job would require commuting to Georgia and re-living the California experience again, but I also saw this as my last opportunity to test this concept. And I had worked on the brand enough to know that the challenges were enormous, yet it was small enough—with a team of people who cared—that it could work.

I knew by then that consulting wouldn't fulfill me. In my work with various organizations, I found that I couldn't really change the lives or trajectories of people or businesses as a contractor. When you're in and out, many people wait until you don't exist anymore and revert to the status quo. Being CEO seemed like the only way to test all my beliefs about running a business, to see if they'd work in "real time."

I sat in that sunroom in Maine, turning over every aspect of the opportunity in my mind.

Is it possible to care deeply about the people while also delivering on the financial and operational requirements?

Will the private equity guys who own the business and Joe have the patience to let this all play out?

So often, people talk about the "right" way to do things, but when you get into the trenches, it just isn't that easy. There are competing dynamics and complexities that make the job much harder than the experts who write books about business make it out to be. In the end, I decided to take the CEO role.

I texted my wife, "I'm gonna call Joe back. I'm gonna tell him I'll do it." Deep down, I needed to know if my approach would actually work in the real world.

Joe and I discussed a potential move to Georgia, but I knew full well that the business was likely to be sold. I couldn't predict what Joe would do in that case, and since he was the only reason I would take on this role, relocation was off the table.

In a short time, I realized we needed some bench strength in finance and sales. I began hiring people who fit the profile necessary to expand the business, providing guidance and watching people grow into their potential, and developing operational controls to help us turn the performance around over time. I was paying attention to both P&Ls: Profit and Loss, and People and Listening.

Very soon after taking over, I found myself intrigued by one employee who served as the liaison of sorts between operations and the plant itself. He appeared to have the skills and capacity to succeed but didn't seem to be responding to the challenges in front of him. After a team video call to address some critical snafus, I could tell he wasn't giving it his all. Though he was leading a vital area of the business—and one facing numerous issues—he was slouched in his chair for the duration of the call. Shortly after, I called him and asked him to come see me.

I used the SBI (Situation, Behavior, Impact) feedback model to guide our discussion. When I expressed what I observed, he said, "What do you mean?"

"Normally you don't see the guy who plays a critical role in an area slouching and looking indifferent on a call," I told him. "Tell me your story."

He looked out the window and then at me. He signed, and sighed, and then he shared it all. He had overcome tremendous challenges and was building a better life for himself. The issue was that the rest of the organization appeared to treat him like the person he had been in the past, not who he had become.

In the process, his dignity and self-worth were being eaten away. How he felt like no one in the company respected him and now knowing his story, I got it. Unfortunately, I'd seen the same scenario play out time and again. Meanwhile, he had too much to offer for me not to invest in him.

When he laid out what he was experiencing, along with a potential solution to the company's situation, I knew that he could help us. We just needed to show we truly valued him and respected him as a human being.

We agreed to a plan, and I told him I'd help—along with another senior leader, whose support I requested. Once we set the plan in motion, I saw an incredible transformation in him and in his ability to work through the complexities necessary to find a more productive solution to the situation.

With those elements in place, the team was able to increase production by 25 percent—without any additional staff. And he did it in record time.

But my own challenges seemed to mount as time went on. Just three months after I arrived, the COVID-19 pandemic hit. The implementation of a new system was becoming daunting as our resources in Europe had to head home in March. I was commuting back and forth between the house in Maine and the company's offices in Georgia. Quarantining between each trip added another layer of complication.

Despite all the challenges, I could feel real change and progress, and our partners in Europe commented on this after the first quarter results. They mentioned that they had seen more progress on the brand in the three short months we had been running it than in the prior years they owned the business.

For the first time, they felt very good about the direction of the business. But they then began to wonder why much of this hadn't been done before our team came onboard. So, they set up calls with me for biweekly discussions about the business.

The calls became increasingly uncomfortable, as they questioned various aspects of the business—including areas I wasn't responsible for. I felt as if I was being put in the middle. It was becoming clearer and clearer to me that this wasn't going to end well, and ultimately I told Joe about it and he stepped in to squash some of the conversations.

Hindsight is always 20/20. I saw that, no matter how much people want to do the right thing and take the right steps forward, politics and personalities always get in the way.

I may have been CEO in title, but I was really just a backup singer in Joe's band, and perhaps rightfully so. He had built an amazing and complex company when no one else was willing to take the same risks or make tough calls. It was a brilliant plan and it was clear that there wasn't room for disruption. Joe knew which strings he wanted to pull. And I certainly knew by then that I didn't want to move to Georgia. Plus, despite the business heading in the right direction, with COVID raging on with no end in sight, there was uncertainty around every corner. And then on September 15th, of 2020, my birthday, Joe came by to see me.

"Let's just end it now," he said and joked that I had lasted longer than most people who had worked for him. Classic Joe for sure.

"I have to tell you, though," Joe said, "The owners think you've done a phenomenal job." He threw a manila folder on my desk, and with that, he left. All I could do was laugh.

I'd expected to be there longer, of course. But in my time at the company, we instituted a complete systems transition, ran the business successfully through the pandemic, and managed to make everyone feel cared for. I also got a chance to see my vision come to life, to battle-test it and learn that it could actually work. I'd met a lot of talented individuals who just needed someone to show they believed in them by treating them with respect and building their skills and confidence. I also learned some things and would certainly change a few decisions, but I think that is true of any situation.

During our first true sales meeting, we created a special award: a superhero cape, to be given to a team member who went above and beyond. Along with the plans I left behind, that became my legacy in a funny way. We equipped people to feel like they could do it. I have heard it has been awarded twice more since my departure, and has become a part of a yearly event. It's something simple yet so powerful—pretty cool.

In the end, I'm proud of the work we did, and proud that I was able to help the team understand that People and Listening were just as important as Profit and Loss, and that both could be prioritized successfully—all while raising people's expectations of themselves and helping them grow personally and professionally.

During one call with the new owners earlier that year, they said, "We see green shoots coming through—shoots we haven't seen since buying the company." I felt that it was a metaphor for my life. When I left, they had hope, and so did I.

* * *

I have always believed that when you declare where you are going in life, people show up. After I left Challenger Turf, two things happened—blessings that helped me learn to trust the journey ahead, this time for good.

Sometime in September 2020, I commented on an article that Bryan Wish wrote and published on LinkedIn. It led to a conversation about how we could work together. And within a week, I received two phone calls from people I'd known for a few years who were interested in my consulting services. They fit the client profile I had developed for Ask Inside: nonprofits or small business leaders who wanted to make an impact.

The opportunities they presented felt like the right decisions at the right time—arriving just as I was working my way through what to do next. I could develop my personal brand, and continue consulting, putting together all I'd learned to follow my path. I knew that with people I trusted and an understanding of the process necessary to tackle any challenge, I could find a way to belong. I could build something powerful and believe in its worth.

Meanwhile, even though I knew consulting wasn't for me, it would pay the bills until I sorted out what I would do long term. Again, I worked with people I knew and liked, and it felt like I was paying them back for all they had done for me. That felt "on brand."

In late September of 2020, I spent some quiet time thinking about what I would do next. But I also knew I needed others' insights to make the right decision. So, I looked to my Personal Trust Community for some perspective. By then I'd learned that sometimes we try to solve it all on our own when others who know us can provide valuable insights. Most of the feedback revolved around living my purpose by coaching in some capacity, versus just consulting. The people who knew me best felt that it was in my DNA. I'd wondered that myself, but never thought it through. As I debated coaching, I reached out to others who were coaching or had done it in the past and learned a great deal about all the options and possibilities.

When it came to coaching and consulting, I had three options: I could operate entirely on my own, running what is called "MasterMinds;" be part of a franchise (T.A.B. was one I considered); or partner with another group (I met with a couple that I could have joined). Then, I heard about Vistage Worldwide.

As I weighed my options, I realized I didn't want to start from scratch. I'd always felt it, but each of these organizations had me take some assessments to see if I would be a good fit. It was obvious when the results came back that I am best when I have the tools and resources to pull from versus starting from scratch. It made sense and it helped me decide what to do next.

I wanted to do the work with tools, experience, and a brand behind me. Vistage—a peer mentoring membership organization for small to mid-size business leaders and executives—seemed like it could be a good option. With a sixty-four-year track record and a library of resources and tools, I could still take the kind of approach I wanted and run things on my terms, but with the support to be successful.

I was also ready to make another change. For years, I had been on the board of the National Council for Adoption. My own adoption had made such an impact on my life, but I'd always been involved in the organization in a passive way. I'd been a committee member for years, but I wasn't committed—just compliant. I determined that I needed to take on a more dynamic role in the organization. I believed in the vision: A world in which all children everywhere have nurturing, permanent families. Now, after so many years and so many different experiences—both personal and professional—I knew I could help bring it to life.

The board had asked me to consider a more active role on multiple occasions. In the past, the timing hadn't been right, or there were board dynamics that wouldn't work for me. I know my limits and my place and it just hadn't been an option. Until right then.

I could share my own adoption story—the one I first opened up about at Yankee Candle, with the help of Dorrin and the Toastmasters—and use my business experience and expertise to further the organization's efforts.

In early fall of 2021, I accepted the role of Chair Elect, with the goal of being chairman at the National Council for Adoption starting in May of 2022.

Our big April fundraising event was held at Nationals Park. As a college baseball player who saw sports as a way to belong, it was a fitting beginning to my new role. And the night itself served as an important opportunity for reflection. The challenges in adoption are tremendous and our ability to equip, educate, and empower those in the adoption community would be our focus moving forward.

At the event, a diverse crowd of supporters shared their stories—from NFL star Demarcus Ware and former Olympic diver and current dog agility trainer Greg Louganis, to *Today's* Hoda Kotb, and former Olympic skater Kitty Carruthers. They told the group about their experiences with adoption—representing a wide variety of perspectives and outcomes.

Standing beside my wife and two of my daughters along with our best friends, the Lemoines, at the reception, I felt proud. I'd hustled to get here, and I'd done it with heart. I'd Belonged, Built, and Believed my way into this role, and honed a community of trusted advisors along the way. I'd developed a sense for how to chart a course forward, and to do it in a way that felt authentic to me.

And finally, I established avenues for others to tell *their* stories, and thus find value in their own experiences—and to understand that people cared. I'd shown them, and myself, that it's worth it.

I hope you'll tell yours. And if you're ready, I'm here to listen.

"Our extended family" including pictures of my parents top middle,
my biological Mom Alice and my biological dad below them.
Little League all stars, A xmas tradition making
cookies, Sarah and I sharing another tradition picking
the xmas tree and running a 5K locally.
On the left is a family photo from a recent wedding of cousins,
below that is one of our cousins on my wife's side, and at
the bottom left is us attending one of Sarah's many musicals
from High School. My biological sister and brother came
along with my folks for this one. It was a special night!
Bottom left was us surprising my mom and dad in Florida
with the family to watch the Red Sox. We got to meet
my dad's favorite player that day, Dustin Pedroia.

Scott and Leslie are in my mom's trusted community and are
the most amazing, caring, and selfless people I know

What I see when I walk into my office in Saco Maine

Maggie, Sarah, and Amanda are attending with me the National Council for Adoption fundraising event at Nationals park. A fitting baseball location for me as I begin my new role as Chairman.

2017 in Washington D.C. meeting with Senator King about policies related to adoption.

EPILOGUE

It was Friday, October 22, 2010. I left work at Yankee Candle in South Deerfield, Massachusetts, and stopped at a convenience store nearby to buy the day's newspaper. It was, after all, my birthday. I also picked up some water and a snack for the ninety-minute ride to Worcester.

About two minutes from my destination, I started getting anxious. I gripped the wheel, my knuckles turning white and palms sweating, and considered turning the car around. But after a few deep breaths, I pressed on.

In the driveway, I parked, grabbed my scrapbook from the passenger seat, and inadvertently left my cell phone behind. At the door, took one more exhale, and knocked.

When it opened, I looked her in the eyes and knew right away: she was my mom. We spent the next five hours catching up on the past forty-six years of my life.

You see, October 22 isn't the day I was born. It's my re-birthday, the day I met my biological family.

After I stepped into her small Worcester home, my biological mother, Alice, introduced me to my three siblings: David, Dwayne, and Kimberly. Dwayne and Kimberly were in sales like I was, and we connected on so many fronts. As we talked, I realized I went to college three miles from where they had lived their whole lives—I'd had no idea.

Further, when I came to understand what Alice had been through over the course of her life, I was blown away by her resilience. She told me about my biological father, Louie, who I'd never meet, and how he was a nomadic individual with a soft spot for helping others. And in learning about them, I finally began to understand who the hell I was.

I scanned the room as everyone was chatting and sharing stories, and realized all those negative thoughts I had about being abandoned as a little boy were so misguided. So many people had shown up for me over the course of my life. I understood how blessed I was to be alive. My mother could have made a very different choice. My adoptive parents could have as well. Moreover, coaches, teachers, mentors, supervisors, friends and—of course—my wife and kids had invested in me. That gave me the courage to start trusting myself inside, to build my Personal Trust Community, to pursue more purposeful work instead of chasing acceptance all the time. Meeting my family of origin was the final piece of the puzzle.

As I got up to leave, I thanked my mother and siblings not just for welcoming me into their home, but for helping me understand who I was. When you know where you come from, it makes it a hell of a lot easier to know where you want to go.

Back into the car, I realized my wife had texted and called me several times while I was inside. Neither my biological family nor I knew what exactly would happen when I knocked on that door and asked for help. But for me, it was exactly the right thing to do.

My experience revealed to me a secret: people actually want to help each other, and the data backs it up. There's a Harvard Business Review article that talks about the warm glow humans get when someone asks them for help. It lifts them out of their own negative state, and fosters connection. Renowned psychologist Heidi Grant says people underestimate others' willingness to help them by over 48 percent! When you say, "I need help," you'll find that you're unleashed from the shackles of your fears and better equipped to reach the next level, whatever that may be.

For all of us, whether in our career, our social life, or our home life, the opportunities to grow as human beings are ever-changing. We're required to regain our sense of belonging all the time: Am I really capable of being a husband? Can I be a father? Can I be a boss? In almost every case, you can. But you can't do it alone. These life transformations require us to have others to help us get where we want to go.

I realized that, for many of us, life is on the other side of that door. But so often, we don't knock.

Why?

We don't believe we're worthy of our own happiness, or we worry that the kind of joy we want just isn't possible. Maybe something happened to us. Maybe that lived experience is holding us back. But when you gather the courage to knock on that door, and it finally opens, you'll find yourself flooded with fulfillment—enough to help you move past your fears and look for the joy and happiness that is within us. What you'll find on the other side, is your own self-worth and dignity.

Sarah Miles, who played Dr. Sharon Fieldstone on Ted Lasso, sums it up best, I believe,

> **"All I try to do is just root my feet and feel like I have a right to be here. I deserve to be loved. I deserve to be seen. I am seen. I am loved."**
> **—Sarah Miles**

Completing a Half Ironman was a great feeling. Suzan Ballmer who has become my Personal Trust Community for my physical well-being was the main reason this happened.

A picture of us on our steps in Saco Maine. I cannot wait for the next chapters in our family and professional lives!

CPSIA information can be obtained
at www.ICGtesting.com
Printed in the USA
LVHW080550010723
751284LV00011BA/185